Values of Harry Potter

www.ValuesOfHarryPotter.com

Values of Harry Potter
Lessons for Muggles
Expanded Edition

Ari Armstrong

Ember Publishing
Denver, Colorado

Copyright © 2008, 2011 by Ari Armstrong
Ember Publishing, Denver, Colorado

Visit www.ValuesOfHarryPotter.com for more information.

Designed by Jennifer Armstrong, www.JenniferLynnArmstrong.com

Armstrong, Ari
Values of Harry Potter: Lessons for Muggles, Expanded Edition
Includes bibliographical information and index
Literary Criticism, Philosophy

ISBN: 978-0-9818030-1-2

Contents

Acknowledgments • 7

Introduction: The Magic of Harry Potter • 9

Part I: Lessons of Harry Potter
Chapter One: The Heroic Fight for Values • 14
Chapter Two: Independence: Mark of the Hero • 28
Chapter Three: Free Will: "It Matters Not
 What Someone Is Born" • 51

Part II: Criticisms of Harry Potter
Chapter Four: The Clash of Love and Sacrifice • 71
Chapter Five: Materialism and Immortality • 86

Conclusion: Mischief Managed • 96

Part III: Additional Essays • 99
The Psychology of Harry Potter • 100
Wizard Law and Segregation • 115
News Media in Harry Potter • 120
Beedle the Bard Expands Rowling's Moral Themes • 131
The Fading Magic of Tolkien and Alexander • 139
Harry Potter's Lessons for Muggle Politicians • 143
Why Potter Fans Should Read Ayn Rand • 146
Reflections on Films Six and Seven • 149

Notes • 155
Index • 169

Acknowledgments

I MIGHT FIRST ACKNOWLEDGE the clever fans of the Harry Potter series who have made it a phenomenon; submitting this modest book for their review makes me feel a bit like Hermione preparing for an O.W.L. Readers are welcome to send me comments about the book at www.ValuesOfHarryPotter.com, where I'll reply to select comments and publish additional articles.

Numerous reviewers offered helpful advice and criticism. My editor, Melissa Holt, reviewed the manuscript with the exactness of Minerva McGonagall. Jennifer Armstrong, my wife, examined drafts at every step, lent me moral support, and designed every aspect of the book; the project would not have been possible without her loving assistance. (Jennifer, a redhead, would be at home in the Weasley household, though she'd have to work on her Quidditch skills.) After looking at very early drafts of the material, Lin Zinser also reviewed the entire manuscript. Darla Graff offered penetrating and detailed notes on most sections that dramatically improved them. Ed Peters double-checked factual claims and citations and also offered general feedback. Craig Biddle, Diana Hsieh, and Brian Schwartz reviewed early drafts of material that eventually became parts of Chapters One, Four, and Five, and Diana also offered useful comments on free will. An anonymous reviewer provided helpful feedback on parts of Chapters One and Four. Readers ought not blame any reviewer for faults in this book, because I stubbornly resisted some of the reviewers' suggestions, and I alone approved the final manuscript. Any remaining errors, whether in fact or logic, are solely my own.

Finally, I thank J. K. Rowling for writing the books that have fascinated and inspired millions of readers around the world and will continue to do so as long as children and youthful spirits yearn for a little magic in their lives.

Introduction
The Magic of Harry Potter

It was the most exciting book buy of my life. My wife and I, along with several family members, went to a bookstore on the evening of July 20, 2007, when stores stayed open late so that they could sell the final Harry Potter novel starting at midnight. Never have I seen any bookstore so packed or heard one so noisy. Gangs dressed as Quidditch players passed by on the sidewalk. Innumerable foreheads sported lightning marks. Children and adults alike drew lots for a place in line to buy the book. The scene was similar in countless bookstores across the nation.

There is no question that J. K. Rowling's Harry Potter books constitute an unprecedented global literary phenomenon. Scholastic, publisher of the books in the United States, announced that the last book sold 8.3 million copies within the first twenty-four hours and 11.5 million in ten days. Combined, the books have sold over 350 million copies worldwide.[1] A Harris Poll suggested that, while the Bible is the favorite book among U.S. readers, "the second choice for 18- to 31-year-olds was J. K. Rowling's Harry Potter series."[2]

Nor does anyone doubt Rowling's profound impact on the reading habits of children. My young cousins, for example, voraciously read each book several times. Parents credit the books for inspiring their children to do better in school.[3] British Chancellor Gordon Brown said, "I think J. K. Rowling has done more for literacy around the world than any single human being."[4] It's difficult to accuse him of exaggeration, if we limit consideration to the modern era.

Yet fierce debate rages over the books. At one end some claim that "the signature of the Prince of Darkness is in these books."[5] In the documentary *Jesus Camp*, a woman speaking to a group of children says, "Had it been in the Old Testament, Harry Potter would have been put to death."[6]

The Vatican has offered a mixed review. Before he became Pope, Joseph Ratzinger warned Catholics to beware the books' "subtle seductions," according to Catholic News Service. More recently, the source reported, "The Vatican newspaper sponsored a face-off between a writer who said the Harry Potter novels offer lessons in the importance of love and self-giving and one who said they teach that with secret knowledge one can control others and the forces of nature."[7]

Obviously, I'm a Potter fan.

I came late to the series, starting after someone gave my wife the first four books in a paperback boxed set. I hold no particular interest in fantasy, and I dismissed Potter as books for kids. But several of my adult friends continually raved about the books, so I thought I'd give them a try.

Quickly I was hooked. What first struck me was the richly dark world of Harry's childhood with his aunt and uncle, Petunia and Vernon Dursley. The idea of escaping from such dreadful circumstances into a bright world of magical heroes fascinated me; it made me think of all the real boys and girls who grow up in similarly bleak circumstances (or worse) and struggle to create a better life for themselves. I hoped that the Potter books comfort those children and motivate adults to help them. Then Rowling took me into an adventure that I enjoyed but did not fully appreciate until I had read further into the series.

By the end of the first book, my respect for the series was sealed with a couple of outstanding quotes by Professor Albus

Dumbledore. "Fear of a name increases fear of the thing itself." "It takes a great deal of bravery to stand up to our enemies, but just as much to stand up to our friends." Yet I was intrigued by some of Dumbledore's other comments that struck me as cryptic. "To the well-organized mind, death is but the next great adventure." "Humans do have a knack of choosing precisely those things [as much money and life as you could want] that are worst for them." "Your mother died to save you." What did Dumbledore mean by these comments? What did they portend for the rest of the series?

Through the first three books, I continued to think of Harry Potter as interesting children's books. Then I read the fourth book, *Harry Potter and the Goblet of Fire*. The main plot, at least until the last few chapters, remains oriented toward children; it involves Harry meeting several challenges in a contest, such as taking an egg from a dragon. More mature themes take on greater significance: the characters deal with bigotry and slavery, the laws of society, and the ethics of journalism. Near the end of the book the forces of evil rise to strength. These are not themes for children, but for maturing youth and adults. The final three books excite youthful spirits, yet the themes grow more complex and at times quite dark, as the villain Lord Voldemort combines qualities of Satan and Hitler.

My book focuses on the heroic fight for values in the Harry Potter series. Harry Potter and his allies struggle valiantly to defend the things that matter to them—their friends, their lives, and their liberty. They do so against great odds, often in agonizing circumstances, and against powerful and relentlessly vicious enemies.

In Chapter One, I review examples illustrating the central theme of the heroic valuer, as contrasted with the motives of the villains.

Chapter Two reviews independence, the virtue that allows the heroes to discover the values that enhance their lives and to pursue them with thoughtful courage.

In Chapter Three, I discuss free will in Harry Potter, the precondition of the selection and pursuit of values.

Chapter Four grows more critical, arguing that Rowling's theme of the heroic valuer ultimately clashes with her secondary theme of Christian self-sacrifice.

Finally, Chapter Five addresses the theme of immortality. How does the quest for earthly immortality motivate the villains? What is the connection between the fear of death, an obsession with objects, and the abuse of others? What does this have to do with the Horcrux? Does virtue require a belief in supernatural immortality? I argue that Rowling does not convincingly develop her theme of immortality or connect it to the motivation of the heroes.

This book presupposes that readers are familiar with the Harry Potter books. The pages that follow discuss crucial elements of plot and will ruin the suspense of the books for those who haven't yet read them.

Much of the fighting over the Potter books involves Christians on both sides, and two of my chapters explicitly deal with Christian themes. Though I am not Christian, and I criticize religion in other forums, I acknowledge that Rowling intentionally includes Christian themes in her books, and I want to understand them correctly. I argue that Rowling's Christian themes of sacrifice and immortality clash with her more central theme of the heroic valuer. I develop my case from the books and outside sources.

My take on the Christian elements of the Potter books conflicts with the perspective of other reviewers. Some argue that the books should be avoided because they oppose Christianity. Others argue that the books should be read and praised because they promote Christian themes. My claim is that the Christian elements of the Potter books are real but disconnected from the broader moral themes of the books, which nevertheless remain brilliant (as Ron Weasley might say).

I compare and contrast some of Rowling's ideas with those of Ayn Rand and Aristotle. Rowling and Rand treat both independence and free will in some strikingly similar ways. Regarding sacrifice, the views of Rowling and Rand clash. On that topic I rely heavily on the writings of Aristotle, whose comments may seem surprising only because they are too often neglected. Rowling and Rand both create vivid heroes who fight for their values, and they again clash on immortality, yet those themes are common enough that I found direct comparisons unnecessary.

Part of my motivation for writing this book is the conviction that the moral lessons of Harry Potter are profoundly important. I made some regrettable moral mistakes as a young adult because I failed to heed some of these lessons, which were widely available long before Rowling conceived Harry Potter. It is vitally important to understand one's values, choose the right values, and enact the virtues that make the achievement of values possible.

While I appreciate Rowling's contribution to a renewal of literacy, I am desperately grateful to her for promoting moral literacy. Adopting the virtues portrayed by the heroes of Harry Potter can make you a better person. Yes, read the books for the sheer joy of the heroic, magical adventure. Then think more deeply about the moral lessons of Harry Potter and strive to integrate them in your day-to-day life. Part of the point of admiring heroes is to become a hero. It's not enough to read about it or write about it; we, all of us, need to live it and face that challenge every day. That is how to discover the true magic of Harry Potter.

Chapter One
The Heroic Fight for Values

Why have J. K. Rowling's books attracted such a devoted following? Much of the success has to do with the vivid alternate reality that Rowling has created with her magical world. Seldom does a reader encounter such richly developed characters; it's hard to read the books and not imagine sitting up in the towers, plotting with Harry Potter or cracking jokes with the Weasley twins. This is particularly true given that Rowling's magical world is written to coexist with our own; readers are tempted to look twice when they see eccentrically dressed people walking down the street who just might be wizards in disguise.

Rowling also has crafted a stunningly intricate plot spanning thousands of pages. While each book contains its independent story, the books also bind together in a grand epic that (including flashbacks) spans decades. Rowling plants deep connections between the books that inspire multiple readings—to take one early example, Hagrid rides into the series on a motorcycle borrowed from Sirius Black, whom we do not meet for another two story-years.

Then there are the subtle references to external works and events ranging from ancient mythology to Christian theology to World War II. Even the names of the characters and the language of the spells provoke research and speculation.

Yet the phenomenal and enduring appeal of the books is due to something more fundamental. What do I remember most vividly about the books? The moments when Harry makes the choice not to put his head down but to face terrifying threats to the people and the life that he loves. Each book reveals such moments.

Harry Potter offers one of literature's great examples of the virtuous hero fighting against the most vicious form of evil. Yes, the vivid storytelling, the intricate plot, and the many layers of allusions place Rowling's series among the grandest and most exciting of epics. But in addition to these elements Rowling does something else particularly well—she shows in passionate detail why victory matters so very much to the heroes.

The overriding theme of the Harry Potter books is the heroic, courageous fight for values. Harry loves his life, loves his friends, loves the magical world in which he lives—and refuses to let go of those values without fighting with all of his strength and resolution.

The budding romances, the school dance, the friendly chats in the halls, the studying and tests, the family dinners, the sports matches—these are not diversions from the central story; they are the reasons why the fight against Voldemort matters. They are the moments of enjoying friends and setting one's course in life. The small moments are not themselves central values, but collectively they manifest such values. Without the heroes' passion for their values expressed in day-to-day living, the stories' detail, plot, and references amount to little.

Harry and his allies feel fear, they suffer pain, and yet always they rise to defend what is important to their lives. They do not ignore the warnings or turn their gaze away; they recognize real dangers to their values and struggle valiantly to overcome those threats.

Harry Potter shows that one must always fight for one's central values, which give life meaning and for which life itself may be risked. Through Harry Potter, Rowling inspires millions of readers to live their lives completely and never willingly surrender their own values.

The Values of the Heroes

What are the central values that Harry and his allies fight to defend?

To grasp why Harry holds his values so intensely, first recall how miserable he is before entering the magical world. Harry is able to see a deep contrast between a life lacking values and a life filled with them.

Until he enters the magical world, Harry lives a deprived life with his awful uncle and aunt, Vernon and Petunia Dursley, and their dreadful son Dudley. The elder Dursleys hated Harry's magical parents, about whom they do not tell him. They resent his magical potential and hide it from him. They underfeed him and force him to sleep beneath the stairs, while spoiling their bratty and manipulative son in equal proportions. "The Dursleys often spoke about Harry…as though he wasn't there—or rather, as though he was something very nasty that couldn't understand them, like a slug." Dudley, picking up his parents' prejudices, leads a little gang in "Dudley's favorite sport: Harry Hunting." Because "Dudley's gang hated that odd Harry Potter in his baggy old clothes and broken glasses," and because the gang terrifies the rest of the students, Harry is friendless at school.

Yet Harry remains open to a life filled with values, and he begins to realize such a life when, on his eleventh birthday, he receives a letter notifying him that he is a wizard who has been accepted into the Hogwarts School of Witchcraft and Wizardry. This opens up a new world for Harry—one in which he is able to discover and actively pursue opulent values.

Even before reaching his new school, Harry finds excellent friends whom he values immensely. Hagrid, the gamekeeper of Hogwarts, delivers Harry's letter of acceptance, offers him heartfelt kindness and gifts, and tells Harry about the wizarding world and his past, including Voldemort's murder of his parents. Harry forms a deep, lasting friendship with Hagrid.

Next Harry meets the Weasley family when Molly, the mother, helps him get onto the train platform for the Hogwarts Express.

The twins, Fred and George, help Harry load his trunk onto the train. And Ronald, with whom Harry shares a train car, becomes Harry's best friend. Eventually the Weasleys practically become Harry's adoptive family. Harry goes on to find many other friends at Hogwarts and among the broader magical community.

Harry soon finds a new home at Hogwarts. He discovers and develops his natural talents, such as flying by broomstick and performing defensive spells. He turns his skills with a broom into success on the Quidditch field. Harry enjoys many of his classes (if not all of them), and he values honing his magical skills and learning extracurricular lessons from Hogwarts.

Harry never takes for granted the things and people that matter to him. Because Harry deeply values his school and friends (and remembers his miserable life before them), he defends these values passionately.

Here we consider three main examples illustrating the basic motives of the heroes, to start with obvious cases that establish the theme before moving on to more difficult examples. (In Chapter Four, where I discuss Christian sacrifice, I review cases in which the heroes' motives are ambiguous and difficult to parse.)

In his first year at Hogwarts, Harry faces the first serious threat to his values. Voldemort, Harry learns, is attempting to steal the Philosopher's Stone (unfortunately called the Sorcerer's Stone in the American editions), which would allow Voldemort to regain his power. Harry's commitment to his values does not waver in the face of danger; Harry decides to try to stop Voldemort.

In persuading his closest friends Ron Weasley and Hermione Granger to join him, Harry points out:

> Voldemort's coming back! Haven't you heard what it was like when he was trying to take over? There won't be any Hogwarts…He'll flatten it, or turn it into a school for the Dark Arts! …D'you think he'll leave you and your families alone…? If I get caught before I can get to the Stone, well, I'll have to go back to the Dursleys and wait for Voldemort to find me there, it's only dying a bit later

than I would have, because I'm never going over to the Dark Side! …Nothing you two say is going to stop me! Voldemort killed my parents, remember?

Harry acts to defend his own life and everything that is important to his life: his liberty, his school, and his friends and other innocents.

Harry's attempted rescue of his godfather Sirius Black in *Order of the Phoenix* again shows Harry courageously defending his values. Harry rushes to save Sirius from Voldemort because Harry loves Sirius. Sirius was best friends with Harry's father and knew Harry as an infant, and he shows deep commitment toward Harry as his godfather. Sirius wishes he could offer Harry a better home, even though he himself must go into hiding. He gives Harry love, fatherly advice, and meaningful gifts, such as Harry's prized flying broomstick. They almost become as father and son.

Near the end of *Order of the Phoenix*, Harry believes, "Sirius is trapped…Voldemort's got him, and no one else knows, and that means we're the only ones who can save him." Harry sets out to save the life of a loved one from Voldemort.

Harry's actions, then, are understandable, but why do his friends—Ginny and Ron Weasley, Hermione, Luna Lovegood, and Neville Longbottom—join him on the dangerous mission to rescue Sirius? They too love their friends and understand the threat that Voldemort poses to all of their values. We look briefly at the motives of each friend in turn.

Ginny has a particular interest in protecting Harry. Aside from her loyalty and affection toward Harry since he saved her life by rescuing her from the monster's den in *Chamber of Secrets*, she has always held a crush for him, which later develops into romance. Ginny too regards Sirius as a friend. And Ginny, who was possessed and nearly killed by Voldemort, knows in a deeply personal way the mayhem that Voldemort threatens to unleash upon her world.

Luna joins Harry because she deeply cares for him and wants to protect her friends from Voldemort. Luna, an eccentric young lady with few friends, holds dear her few excellent companions.

While Luna also recognizes the broader threat that Voldemort poses, perhaps her deepest concern is for the safety of these particular friends, who mean the world to her. It is only later, when Harry learns that Luna has been kidnapped, that he fully appreciates how much Luna values her friends—she has lovingly painted highly detailed portraits of them.

Neville joins Harry because, perhaps more than any of the other friends, he understands Voldemort's destructive potential and knows the villain must be stopped. Like Harry, Neville suffered great personal loss at the hands of Voldemort, whose followers tortured Neville's parents to insanity. Neville, too, recognizes Voldemort's power to destroy his values.

Moreover, Neville regards Harry as a dear friend as well as a critical ally in the fight against Voldemort, so Neville wants to keep Harry safe. Harry has always looked out for Neville. Even though Neville is at times socially awkward, Harry stands up for him against the school bully, Draco Malfoy, during their first flying lesson. Later, when Draco places a curse on Neville, Ron encourages, "You've got to stand up to him, Neville!" In response to Neville's concern that he's not brave enough, Harry says, "You're worth twelve of Malfoy." When Draco tells Neville he's "got no brains," Neville invokes Harry's words against Draco and joins Ron in fighting him. Neville, then, helps Harry because he values him tremendously as a friend. Neville also realizes that Harry holds power against Voldemort and therefore is an invaluable ally who must be protected.

Ron and Hermione stand by Harry as they have in the past. The friends hate Voldemort and want to thwart him, and they value Harry as a brave, virtuous, and loyal companion. Recall, for example, that early in their first year, Harry and Ron rush to rescue Hermione from an escaped troll. The three develop a very deep love for each other as friends and thus are prepared to do whatever it takes to protect each other from harm. It is no surprise that his friends join Harry on a dangerous mission to save Sirius and, later, to battle against Voldemort. Each has a personal stake in the outcome.

Outside of Harry's schoolmates, Dobby, a house-elf, offers another clear example of a character who fights to protect what is dear to him. Why does Dobby put himself at great personal risk and incur painful injuries to help Harry throughout the books?

House-elves have been forced into slavery and are used to being treated viciously. Dobby held Harry as a hero even before the two met, Dobby explains, because the infant Harry defeated Voldemort and now stands against his return to power:

> Ah, if Harry Potter only knew...what he means to us, to the lowly, the enslaved, we dregs of the magical world! Dobby remembers how it was when [Voldemort] was at the height of his powers, sir! We house-elfs were treated like vermin, sir! Of course, Dobby is still treated like that...But mostly, sir, life has improved for my kind since you triumphed over [Voldemort]. Harry Potter survived, and the Dark Lord's power was broken, and it was a new dawn, sir, and Harry Potter shone like a beacon of hope for those of us who thought the Dark days would never end.

Thus Dobby goes out of his way to protect Harry, and he continues to find new reasons to regard Harry as his dearest ally. Early in *Chamber of Secrets*, Dobby tries to sabotage Harry's efforts to return to school in order to protect Harry from Dobby's malicious master, Lucius Malfoy (Draco's father). The magical bonds of slavery force Dobby to hurt himself for this. At their first meeting, Harry politely asks Dobby to sit on his bed. Dobby "burst into tears," explaining, "Dobby has *never* been asked to sit down by a wizard—like an *equal*." Later, when Harry tricks Lucius into freeing Dobby from his service to the Malfoys, Dobby recognizes the great deed Harry has done for him.

By the final book, Dobby becomes a central hero of the series when he rescues Harry and his friends from the clutches of Voldemort's followers—again putting himself at risk and this time falling on the tragic side of luck. Yet to Dobby the risk was worth it, for in defending Harry Potter and his allies, Dobby defends everything that is good about his own life.

The Villains

It is clear that Harry Potter and his allies generally act to defend their personal values. What, then, motivates the villains of the story?

Slytherin is one of the four Hogwarts houses named after the founders of the school. Before placing students in their houses, the Sorting Hat describes Slytherin, through which Voldemort and most of his followers passed, as "cunning folk [who] use any means / To achieve their ends." Before placing Harry in Gryffindor, the house known for bravery, the Sorting Hat tells Harry that "Slytherin will help you on the way to greatness, no doubt about that."

However, the villains do not, in fact, attain greatness, nor do they achieve any ends worth wanting. While Harry and his allies heroically defend the values dear to them, all the villains achieve is misery and self-destruction.

In the first book, Professor Quirrell, who has been secretly working to help Voldemort recover the Philosopher's Stone, tells Harry: "There is no good and evil, there is only power, and those too weak to seek it." Yet Quirrell admits that he fares poorly under this sort of power. He says, shivering, "[Voldemort] has had to be very hard on me. ...He does not forgive mistakes easily. When I failed to steal the stone [previously], he was most displeased. He punished me."

In the case of the Philosopher's Stone, who has actually achieved life-enriching values? On one hand, Harry and his friends undertake a difficult, risky, and painful quest to prevent Voldemort from gaining the Stone—in order to protect all that they cherish. Quirrell, on the other hand, has made himself the servant of a vicious wizard who tortures him, alienating himself from all love, friendship, and other requirements of genuine happiness. It is Quirrell who destroys all of his potential values, surrendering not only his mind but his physical body to Voldemort. Quirrell serves as the bodily host for Voldemort's twisted soul, which is all that remains after the wizard's prior defeat. Ultimately, Voldemort "left Quirrell to die."

Prisoner of Azkaban reveals a similar example. Harry's godfather Sirius, long imprisoned for a crime he did not commit, confronts Peter Pettigrew, the man who betrayed Harry and his parents to Voldemort. Sirius accuses: "You never did anything for anyone unless you could see what was in it for you. …You'd want to be quite sure [Voldemort] was the biggest bully in the playground before you went back to him, wouldn't you?"

The cowardly Pettigrew eventually admits his vile deeds. He offers an excuse: Voldemort "was taking over everywhere! …What was there to be gained by refusing him?"

Sirius answers him: "What was there to be gained by fighting the most evil wizard who has ever existed? …Only innocent lives, Peter!" Pettigrew responds, "You don't understand! …He would have killed me, Sirius!" Sirius is unsympathetic: "Then you should have died! Died rather than betray your friends, as we would have done for you!"

Is it true that Pettigrew gains personally by turning over his friends to Voldemort? Pettigrew loses all of his friends to prostrate himself before a vicious master. With Voldemort's initial defeat, Pettigrew must transform into a rat and live that way for years. Once he rejoins Voldemort, he lives in a state of perpetual terror. Voldemort, in regaining his body, forces Pettigrew to chop off his own hand for use in the transformation. As Voldemort toys with the mortified Pettigrew, the traitor is reduced to "uncontrollable weeping." Voldemort finally gives him a new hand—which later strangles him to death. Pettigrew exchanges all of his values for a pitiful and brief existence of misery, isolation, terror, pain, and servility.

Had Pettigrew tried to resist Voldemort, Dumbledore's supporters, the Order of the Phoenix, might have been able to protect him. Pettigrew could have fought against Voldemort, increasing the chances of taking him down earlier. If Voldemort killed Pettigrew—as he does in the end anyway—at least Pettigrew could have died fighting for values that gave his life meaning.

What Pettigrew tragically fails to realize, as Sirius succinctly states later on, is that "there are things worth dying for." That is, there are things worth risking one's life to defend—because life without them isn't worth living.

Another example of the self-destructiveness of following Voldemort comes from *Half-Blood Prince*, in which Draco Malfoy's mother, Narcissa, visits Professor Severus Snape. Narcissa believes that Snape too is loyal to Voldemort, but Snape is actually working as a spy for Dumbledore, whom Voldemort has ordered Draco to murder. Narcissa rightly believes that Voldemort assigned Draco this impossibly dangerous task so that he would be killed in the process of attempting it. Voldemort does this to punish the elder Malfoys for failing to carry out one of Voldemort's previous plans. Narcissa asks Snape to help Draco. "My son…my only son," she pleads. Snape replies, "The Dark Lord is very angry…You know as well as I do, Narcissa, that he does not forgive easily." Serving Voldemort poses a threat to one's own life and every value that promotes it.

Indeed, even to give Voldemort bad news can be a death warrant. When he learns that Harry has stolen an object that contains a piece of his soul, Voldemort takes out his rage on several of his followers, including Lucius Malfoy and Bellatrix Lestrange, who is Voldemort's most loyal surviving supporter. The pair barely escape with their lives, while "those who were left were slain, all of them, for bringing him this news."

What about Voldemort himself? Does he live a happy life enriched with values? Dumbledore tells Harry that, even as a youth, Voldemort had "obvious instincts for cruelty…and domination. …Lord Voldemort has never had a friend." While Harry's life is filled with friends and loved ones, Voldemort's life is devoid of such values.

Moreover, Voldemort performs horrendous acts of evil, twisting his soul beyond recognition as human. When Voldemort slays a unicorn to drink its sustaining blood, he achieves only "a half-life, a cursed life," as a centaur explains to Harry. Voldemort commits many murders, and as Harry learns, Voldemort's dark magic leads to a depraved existence worse than death. Killing "is an act of violation…Killing rips the soul apart." Dumbledore notes that "Lord Voldemort has seemed to grow less human with the passing years," his soul "mutilated beyond the realms of…'usual evil.'"

Nor does Voldemort ultimately achieve the power over others that he seeks. After his power is destroyed by the infant Harry, Voldemort lives a shadowy existence, barely alive. When he regains his power, much of the wizarding world again fights against him, trying desperately to destroy him. Finally, Harry and his allies succeed in the task.

Voldemort and his followers abuse and seek to control others, and in doing so they undermine their own life-promoting values. Harry and his allies fight for and usually achieve a life filled with joy, happiness, friendship, love, and worthwhile pursuits. Voldemort and his followers achieve for themselves pain, suffering, fear, alienation, and in many cases death.

The contrast between the heroes and the villains illustrates the nature of values. At the simplest level, values are the things a person goes after and wants to get, achieve, or protect. However, such a limited concept doesn't explain the differences between Harry and Voldemort. If Harry values friends, his liberty, a pleasant meal, Quidditch, and his wand, Voldemort values power and inflicting pain. In the broader sense, values must genuinely contribute to one's life, and they must be attainable without destroying the rest of one's values. Friendship in fact contributes to Harry's well-being and happiness and supports his other values. Inflicting pain in fact makes Voldemort a despicable wretch who systematically destroys everything that makes life worth living. In the broad sense, then, a value is not merely something that one goes after; it is something worth going after. I refer to values in that broad sense.

Values in the Face of Death

Harry Potter and his allies fight for their values, while the villains act to destroy their own values. This basic theme of Harry Potter illuminates more difficult cases.

At times the heroes put their lives at extreme risk. However, generally they do so in order to defend their own values. Risking one's life for one's values is the ultimate form of fighting for values. While nobody hopes to be placed in such circumstances—and while, thankfully, they are extremely rare in the free world outside of wartime—when a life-threatening danger emerges, the heroic valuer finds the courage to confront the danger.

The books revolve around three momentous acts in which characters put their lives on the line. When Voldemort attacks the infant Harry, Lily gives her life to save her son, and this is the "ancient magic" that first defeats Voldemort. In *Half-Blood Prince*, Dumbledore gives his life to save a student and protect Snape (who is working undercover against Voldemort). In the final book, Harry offers his life to save his friends and destroy Voldemort. Let us consider these examples in turn.

Voldemort kills Harry's mother because he hears of a prophecy that predicts a newborn boy will grow up to threaten his power. Voldemort intuits that this boy is Harry, the son of James and Lily Potter. Voldemort murders James and Lily and attempts to murder Harry. Lily dies protecting her infant son.

Dumbledore explains to Harry why Voldemort could not kill him as an infant and why Harry continues to find protection with his mother's family. "You [are] protected by an ancient magic…I am speaking, of course, of the fact that your mother died to save you. She gave you a lingering protection…that flows in your veins to this day. …Her blood became your refuge."

Any decent parent, and anyone who has seriously contemplated parenthood, recognizes the supreme value that is one's own children. Lily loves her son more than anything, and she does what any normal parent would do: she tries to protect her child from a murderer. Lily begs Voldemort, "Not Harry, please no, take me, kill me instead." Voldemort "could have forced her away from the crib, but it seemed more prudent to finish them all."

Even if Lily had not tried desperately to save the life of her son, she still would have been killed. Had she escaped Voldemort on that night, her life would have been in constant danger, as Voldemort is a ruthless killer.

More importantly, if Lily had failed to take every possible action in defense of her son, her highest value, she would have lived in constant agony had she lived and Harry died. For her own sake, Lily had to defend Harry. Even though the effort appeared hopeless, the alternative was unthinkable. Only one choice was open to Lily with any conceivable chance of protecting her values.

Dumbledore's death, the second major example, is described near the end of *Half-Blood Prince*. When Draco confronts Dumbledore with the intention of killing him, Dumbledore recognizes that Voldemort has threatened to kill Draco and his entire family should he fail. Finally, Draco cannot bring himself to kill his headmaster. Dumbledore begs Snape to do it instead.

Dumbledore takes this extreme action to protect his values. As headmaster of Hogwarts, Dumbledore has pledged himself to the instruction and safety of his pupils, and Draco, a troubled young man but not one beyond hope, remains one of Dumbledore's students. Dumbledore is committed to his work—his work is his life—and he could not bear to allow Draco's soul to be "ripped apart" through an act of murder. By allowing Snape to kill him, Dumbledore not only protects Draco from spiritual destruction and certain death at the hands of Voldemort, but also maintains Snape's role as a spy, enabling Snape ultimately to help bring down the vicious tyrant.

What are Dumbledore's alternatives? Dumbledore is severely injured, and it is unclear whether he could have successfully fought Voldemort's followers even if he had tried. Dumbledore knows that, by failing to protect Snape's role as a spy, the world that he values likely would continue to crumble around him. Moreover, when Dumbledore asks Snape to kill him, he knows that, owing to a previous injury, he has only months to live anyway. Dumbledore chooses a moment's satisfaction knowing that he is protecting Draco, Snape, and the rest of his values. His alternative is to betray the role of headmaster that he loves and then spend several months of physical and emotional agony as his body and entire world fall apart.

Turning to the final case, Harry apparently must die because, as Dumbledore explains to Snape, when Voldemort tried to kill Harry "a fragment of Voldemort's soul...latched itself onto" him. "And while that fragment of soul...remains attached to and protected by Harry, Lord Voldemort cannot die." Upon hearing this, Harry believes that "he was not supposed to survive." Harry, thinking that Voldemort will live so long as Harry does, marches off willingly to meet his death.

What is the alternative? So long as Voldemort lives, neither Harry nor any of his loved ones are safe. His choice is death, knowing in the process that his action will save everyone else he loves, or the likelihood of a short and painful life during which he gets to watch his loved ones murdered around him. Notably, Harry does not put his life on the line for his enemies or even for nameless strangers, but rather for his friends and allies; when contemplating his fate he remembers a kiss with his beloved.

Moreover, Harry does not die but rather kills off the part of Voldemort's soul trapped inside of him (by surviving Voldemort's curse) so that he can finally defeat the monster. Dumbledore suspected all along that Voldemort would not really be able to kill Harry, again because of the protection of his mother's final act of love. Even though Harry was convinced he was headed for death, the event shows that such courageous actions can succeed. Though Harry's success in the story is facilitated by magic, his success mirrors real-world cases of courageous triumph in the face of seemingly overwhelming odds.

It is precisely because Rowling shows vivid characters fighting tenaciously for their values that her books are so compelling. Her books will inspire generations of readers to reach for the strength and moral courage to defend the values that make their lives worth living.

Now that we have explored the central theme of the heroic valuer, we turn in Chapter Two to a discussion of independence, a virtue necessary for the achievement of values.

Chapter Two

Independence: Mark of the Hero

AMONG THE MORAL THEMES of the Harry Potter books is the recognition of the value of independence in thinking and acting. Independence in this context means relying upon one's own reasoning mind to reach decisions in consideration of the relevant facts and then acting for values consistent with such judgments. The opposite of independence is to profess beliefs and take actions not because they are true and right, but because of what other people think.

Independence does not mean ignoring others, disdaining them, avoiding their company, or rejecting their help. Indeed, those who think and act independently put themselves in an excellent position to develop valuable relationships with others; the heroes of J. K. Rowling's books develop deep friendships and loyalties. Those who place their minds and values at the mercies and whims of others, on the other hand, tend to relate to others based on social pressures or considerations of status. Thus, independence is not about whether one has friends; it is about whether one approaches all of life, including relationships with others, according to one's own considered judgment of the facts.

Another way to describe independence is thinking and acting in accordance with one's first-handed understanding. Yes, one can learn and gain values from others, but only by reaching one's own honest judgment about such knowledge and benefits.

Second-handers, then, are those who accept claims because of social pressure or status or a misplaced trust in authority. (For the classic treatment of the first-hander versus the second-hander, see Ayn Rand's 1943 novel *The Fountainhead*.[8]) An independent, first-handed thinker defies the opinions of crowds and authorities when they contradict known facts and reasoned beliefs.

Second-handers try to gain values as well as knowledge through a misplaced reliance on others. For example, second-handers will claim to want something just because it's popular, or they will try to get something by manipulating or coercing the opinions of others. The independent actor, by contrast, holds first-handed values and seeks to influence others solely by honest persuasion, in accordance with the other person's own independent, first-handed understanding.

Rowling presents many positive examples of independence and many negative examples of second-handedness, which comes in many variants. After considering how second-handers attempt to gain social standing and power in the novels, we will look at the alternative of independence that characterizes the actions of the heroes. The examples provided by the books illustrate the nature and problems of the second-hander as well as the virtues of the first-handed heroes.

Second-Handers and Social Standing

Early in his life, Harry witnesses the second-handed behavior of the Dursleys, who despise the magical and strange Potters. Both Vernon and Petunia orient themselves primarily toward their neighbors.

Vernon becomes enraged merely to see people (wizards, in fact) wearing "funny clothes." When he hears some of these wizards mention Harry's name, he tries to pretend that this can't be his nephew. Vernon hopes he is "imagining things, which he had never hoped before, because he didn't approve of imagination."

He tries to wish away anything outside of "normal" behavior, but he disdains wishing or hoping for anything beyond social expectations.⁹

Meanwhile, Petunia concerns herself with "Mrs. Next Door's problems." Later, "Uncle Vernon, Aunt Petunia, and Dudley had gone out into the front garden to admire Uncle Vernon's new company car (in very loud voices, so that the rest of the street would notice it too)."

When Harry was an infant and still living with his parents, Petunia "pretended she didn't have a sister, because her sister and her good-for-nothing husband were as unDursleyish as it was possible to be." And what does it mean to be "Dursleyish"? It means to conform to the standards and expectations of one's neighbors, to be "perfectly normal." "The Dursleys shuddered to think what the neighbors would say if the Potters arrived in the street."

Unfortunately for the Dursleys' comfortably normal life, Voldemort murders Harry's parents, and the infant Harry goes to live with the Dursleys. How do Vernon and Petunia react to Harry's magical potential? "We swore…we'd stamp it out of him!" To the Dursleys, Harry's ability is an "abnormality." The Dursleys' attitude toward Harry does not change even after Harry enters the magical world; having failed to "squash the magic out of him… they lived in terror of anyone finding out that Harry had spent most of the last two years at Hogwarts."

Squashing the magic out of Harry means giving him as little food and possessions as possible and berating him constantly. Meanwhile, the Dursleys encourage their own son to view possessions as means to show up and manipulate others. Though Dudley's parents shower their son with gifts, Dudley doesn't appreciate these gifts, and he proceeds to destroy them. Dudley does not much enjoy the gifts themselves; he enjoys forcing others to give him more than other people get.

Petunia calls her sister Lily a freak, strange and abnormal. Petunia laments that, for her parents, "it was Lily this and Lily that." A memory from Petunia's childhood reveals the origins of her envy: she, too, wanted to attend Hogwarts and learn magic, but she was not born with any magical ability. Rather than develop her own talents and relationship with her parents, Petunia wanted the opportunities and attention that her sister had. (The books suggest no reason to think that the girls' parents were any less supportive of Petunia, but clearly she wanted the advantages of her sister.) Whether trying to get what her sister has or calling her sister a freak, Petunia focuses on her status in the eyes of other people rather than her own goals and values.

Soon after Harry enters the magical world he meets Draco, another second-hander. Draco, in bragging about his possessions, reminds Harry of Dudley. Draco too sees possessions primarily as symbols of social status. He immediately dismisses Harry's first friend of the magical world, Hagrid, as "a sort of servant." Draco also asks Harry whether his parents are magical. Draco says, "I really don't think they should let the other sort in, do you?"

As Petunia is prejudiced against those who can do magic, Draco is prejudiced against those born of Muggles, or non-magical parents. While Petunia fears that associating with the magical world will reduce her status in the eyes of her "normal" neighbors, Draco holds that associating with Muggles and Muggle-born magical students reduces the status of established magical lines. Both Petunia and Draco judge people according to social status rather than as individuals.

In *Chamber of Secrets*, Rowling introduces an archetype of the second-hand mentality: Gilderoy Lockhart. This new Hogwarts professor surrounds himself with pictures of…himself. When he first sees Harry at a book-signing event, Lockhart drags Harry in front of the cameras, saying, "Nice big smile, Harry… Together, you and I are worth the front page." This exemplifies the relationship between narcissism and second-handedness: the narcissist is infatuated with his own image as measured by the standards of others.

Lockhart constantly reminds others of his fame, including his many awards. On the first day of class, he gives his students a test covering personal details about himself as revealed in his many books. When Harry must serve detention with Lockhart, the professor has Harry help him answer fan mail. "Celebrity is as celebrity does, remember that," Lockhart says. Yet Lockhart's celebrity is no substitute for real ability.

Lockhart constantly brags about his skills, which he is never able to demonstrate. On one occasion, Lockhart unintentionally removes all the bones from Harry's arm while trying to heal it; another time, he tries to make a snake disappear but only makes it larger.

Finally, Lockhart proves his cowardice in trying to avoid helping to rescue Ginny when she is trapped in the monster's chamber. Harry reminds Lockhart of all the brave things he reported doing in his books. Lockhart admits to Harry, "My dear boy…Do use your common sense. My books wouldn't have sold half as well if people didn't think *I'd* done all those things. No one wants to read about some ugly old Armenian warlock, even if he did save a village from werewolves."

Shocked, Harry questions, "So you've just been taking credit for what a load of other people have done?" Lockhart admits his lies and then tries to wipe Harry's mind of the conversation. Lockhart fails and in the process removes his own memory, reducing himself to helplessness. Lockhart's case demonstrates the ultimate futility and self-destructiveness of living for the empty approval of others, rather than for one's own authentic knowledge and values.

The Temptation of Second-Handedness

Rowling shows that basically good people, even heroes, can sometimes succumb to second-handedness. The clearest example of this is Remus Lupin, the professor who replaces Lockhart for Harry's third year at Hogwarts.

Lupin is unusual because, as a child, he was bitten by a werewolf, thus becoming one himself. He changes into a wolf a few nights each month, when his bite would turn others into werewolves. Fortunately, he can control his transformations using a magical potion created for this purpose. Though Lupin poses no threat to others (unless unable to take the potion on time), he recognizes that most people will never accept a werewolf as an equal. Once his condition becomes known, Lupin, among Harry's best teachers, resigns from the school to avoid parental outrage over a werewolf teaching their children. Harry and Lupin remain close; Lupin was best friends in school with Harry's father and godfather, and Harry joins Lupin in the Order of the Phoenix, the organization formed to battle Voldemort.

Harry wonders why another member of the Order, Nymphadora Tonks, has fallen into poor spirits. Eventually he realizes that it is because she is in love with Lupin, who initially spurns her attentions because he wants to spare her the problems of being involved with a werewolf. Tonks returns to her usual happy nature when she announces her marriage with Lupin.

Lupin regrets his decision to marry Tonks. Leaving his now-pregnant wife with her parents, Lupin offers to travel with Harry. Lupin claims that Harry's father would have wanted it that way. Harry sees through this pretext. He retorts, "I'm pretty sure my father would have wanted to know why you aren't sticking with your own kid, actually." Lupin replies:

> I made a grave mistake in marrying Tonks...Don't you understand what I've done to my wife and my unborn child? I should never have married her, I've made her an outcast! ...You don't know how most of the Wizarding world sees creatures like me! When they know of my affliction, they can barely talk to me! ...Even her own family is disgusted by our marriage, what parents want their only daughter to marry a werewolf? ...And if, by some miracle, [my child] is not like me, then it will be better off...without a father of whom it must always be ashamed!

Harry is unsympathetic. He realizes that Lupin is playing into the irrational prejudices that others hold against him. Harry says, "I'd never have believed this...The man who taught me to fight dementors—a coward." Harry's words sting, but they work.

Lupin returns to Tonks. Later, when Lupin announces the birth of his son, he asks Harry to be godfather. Although he succumbs to second-handed thinking for a time, Lupin realizes that he must not put social pressure or the views of others above doing what is right for himself and his family.

Second-Handers and Power

At first glance, those who seek the approval of others and those who seek power over others might seem to be opposites. Approval-seekers grovel for attention and for the favor of others; they prostrate themselves to the views of others. Power-seekers, on the other hand, want to exercise power over others and force others to do their bidding. Yet in both cases, the primary orientation is toward *other people*. Neither the approval-seeker nor the power-seeker focuses on his own knowledge of what is true and right or on his own achievement of values. Both types of second-handers rely fundamentally on other people; they are basically dependent on the views and position of others.

A good example of a power-seeking second-hander is Percy Weasley, Ron's older brother. Percy is not viciously evil, as are the main villains, yet he creates serious problems for himself and for others—notably, his family—through his preoccupation with political power.

In Harry's second year at Hogwarts, Percy serves as prefect, a student leader of the school. Ron finds him "deeply immersed in a small and deeply boring book called *Prefects Who Gained Power*." Ron mocks, "Percy, he's got it all planned out…He wants to be Minister of Magic." There's nothing inherently wrong with holding a position of responsibility, political or otherwise. Percy's main motivation, however, is not to find work in which he can enjoy using his talents toward a useful goal, but to find a position that grants him social prestige and command.

Once Percy graduates from school, he enters the Ministry of Magic. When his boss, Barty Crouch, Sr., discovers his house-elf Winky (whom we will consider in more detail later) at the scene of a crime, Crouch punishes the elf even without good evidence that she was involved. Percy defends the move on the grounds of public appearance: "Well, Mr. Crouch is quite right to get rid of an elf like that! …Running away when he'd expressly told her not to…embarrassing him in front of the whole Ministry…how would that have looked, if she'd been brought up in front of [a board]?" For Percy, the way things appear to others is more important than the truth.

Because Percy places appearance before facts and seeks power, he covers for Crouch even when Crouch stops performing his job. As another of Ron's brothers explains, others in the Ministry of Magic "said Percy ought to have realized Crouch was off his rocker and informed a superior. But you know Percy, Crouch left him in charge, he wasn't going to complain." For the same reason, Percy does not question why the Minister of Magic, Cornelius Fudge, asks Percy to join his office. The same brother intuits the reason: "Fudge only wants Percy in his office because he wants to use him to spy on the family." By this time, the rest of the Weasleys have joined the Order of the Phoenix, while the Ministry of Magic has refused to recognize Voldemort's return to strength. Because Percy is a second-hander, all he accomplishes (besides alienating his entire family and his virtuous friends) is to impede the fight against Voldemort.

Percy is not the only member of the Ministry of Magic preoccupied with power and appearance. Fudge, the Minister, chooses to ignore the abundant evidence of Voldemort's return to power and his attempts to assert control over the wizarding world.

Dumbledore warns Fudge that he must take immediate action to counter Voldemort. Fudge refuses to believe the facts. Instead, Fudge accuses, "It seems to me that you are all determined to start a panic." Fudge is more concerned about public reaction to the news than whether the news is true.

Dumbledore tries in vain to get Fudge "to send envoys to the giants" before Voldemort can bring them to his side. Fudge responds: "If the magical community got wind that I had approached the giants—people hate them, Dumbledore—end of my career."

Dumbledore returns: "You are blinded...by the love of the office you hold, Cornelius!" Dumbledore also points out to Fudge that he panders to and adopts common prejudices: "You place too much importance...on the so-called purity of blood!" Fudge weakly calls Dumbledore's warnings "insane." Fudge cannot see past his second-handed orientation toward the perception of others. For Fudge, all that is important is that he remain in power and not disrupt popular opinions, however misguided they might be.

In his desperation to cling to power, Fudge only becomes more paranoid—and more dangerous. Before Harry enters his fifth year, Fudge "absolutely refus[es]" to believe that Voldemort has returned to strength. Why? Arthur Weasley, Ron's father, explains, "You see, Fudge thinks Dumbledore's plotting to overthrow him. He thinks Dumbledore wants to be Minister of Magic." Ridiculously, Fudge believes that all of the claims about Voldemort are part of a conspiracy to undermine his authority and position.

What's more, in order to suppress the truth about Voldemort, Fudge turns to censorship. Lupin tells Harry that "the Ministry's leaning heavily on the *Daily Prophet* not to report any of what they're calling Dumbledore's rumor-mongering, so most of the wizarding community are completely unaware anything's happened, and that makes them easy targets for" Voldemort's followers.

The effort to control the opinions of others through deception is a different twist for the second-hander. Vernon Dursley accepts the beliefs of his neighbors as an absolute and deceives himself to bring his own beliefs into line with those of others. Fudge does the same thing in some situations, but here his lust for power drives him not only to deceive himself but also to try to control the opinions of others and bring popular attitudes into line with his own.

Fudge and the Order contrast sharply. Dumbledore and his allies seek to persuade others through facts and reason so they can understand firsthand the danger Voldemort poses. Fudge tries to manipulate his own beliefs and the beliefs of others. Harry and his allies hold facts as primary. Fudge places opinions before facts.

The first-hander seeks to bring his beliefs into line with the truth and with legitimate values. The second-hander treats facts and values as a matter of others' opinion. Whether second-handers try to conform to or manipulate the opinions of others, the second-hander's primary concern is the beliefs of other people, without regard for the legitimacy of those beliefs.

Because Fudge refuses to accept facts, he creates a political environment of fear, intimidation, and caprice. At a hearing intended to silence Harry through trumped-up charges, Fudge falsely calls Harry a liar. Dumbledore reminds Fudge that "the Ministry does not have the power to expel Hogwarts students" or "to confiscate wands until charges have been successfully proven." Fudge retorts, "Laws can be changed."

Unsurprisingly, Fudge's paranoia, refusal to acknowledge facts, and incompetence eventually cost him his job, once Voldemort's return becomes too obvious for even him to ignore. Fudge's replacement, Rufus Scrimgeour, handles the job with greater skill, but he, too, tries to manipulate the opinions of others. Scrimgeour tells Harry:

> It's all perception, isn't it? It's what people believe that's important. …They think you are quite the hero…You might consider it…almost a duty, to stand alongside the Ministry, and give everyone a boost. …If you were to be seen popping in and out of the Ministry from time to time…that would give the right impression.

Harry sees through Scrimgeour's flattery: "So basically…you'd like to give the impression that I'm working for the Ministry?" Harry throws the offer in Scrimgeour's face:

> You see, I don't like some of the things the Ministry's doing. Locking up Stan Shunpike [who is known to be innocent], for instance. …You're making Stan a scapegoat, just like you want to make me a mascot. …Either we've got Fudge, pretending everything's lovely while people get murdered right under his nose, or we've got you,

chucking the wrong people into jail and trying to pretend you've got [me] working for you!

Harry recognizes the error of trying to manipulate the opinions of others through pretense, whatever its form. Whether Fudge tries to convince people that there is no danger, or Scrimgeour tries to convince people that he's arresting dangerous criminals or working with a powerful ally, such pretense rests on the view that most important is what other people believe, not the facts.

A particularly wicked example of a power-seeking secondhander is Dolores Umbridge, who takes Fudge's policy of manipulating opinions to ghastly levels.

Fudge assigns Umbridge to Hogwarts to silence talk of Voldemort, monitor the other staff members, and prevent students from learning magic that they might use to undermine Fudge's power. She even physically abuses Harry for speaking up about Voldemort by forcing Harry to write lines with a magic pen that makes his hand bleed. Umbridge prevents her students from learning defensive magic because, as Sirius explains, Fudge fears that Dumbledore is "forming his own private army, with which he will be able to take on the Ministry of Magic." Eventually, Fudge grants Umbridge more power over the school by making her "High Inquisitor." As Umbridge grows more tyrannical at Hogwarts, Voldemort breaks his followers out of Azkaban and brings the prison's ghoulish guards—the dementors—under his control.

Umbridge is particularly nasty toward Harry as she attempts to shut him up. Umbridge first appears at Harry's hearing, where she challenges Dumbledore. Harry has been charged with using magic as a minor outside of school, which is forbidden. However, the reason that Harry used magic was to defend himself and Dudley Dursley from dementors. Dumbledore wonders why dementors, supposedly under Ministry control, attacked Harry. Umbridge mocks Dumbledore for this and encourages other members of the council to join her in making fun of Dumbledore. Thus, Umbridge helps Fudge in his efforts to discredit Dumbledore and Harry.

Harry later learns that Umbridge knew all along who ordered the dementors to attack: she did. Finally she admits that Fudge "never knew I ordered dementors after Potter last summer, but he was delighted to be given the chance to expel him, all the same." The fact that dementors enjoy destroying their victims caused Umbridge no hesitation.

In this case, Umbridge reveals her second-handedness in several ways. Even though she acted independently of Fudge's knowledge, such independence is superficial and based on her subservience to an authority. She accepts the authority of Fudge and the Ministry of Magic, and she therefore acts to suppress the facts about Voldemort; even though she does not tell Fudge about the dementors, she sends them based on Fudge's official line. She also uses violence (as well as deception and intimidation) against others in order to compel their actions—a theme to which we will return.

As Umbridge accepts the authority of the ministry, so she insists that her students accept what an authority tells them. When Hermione asks why they are not learning to use defensive spells, Umbridge responds with condescension: "Are you a Ministry-trained educational expert…? Wizards much older and cleverer than you have devised our new program of study." When Harry points out that the students need to learn defensive magic to protect themselves from Voldemort and his followers, Umbridge calls Harry a liar. Harry retorts, "I saw him, I fought him!" But Umbridge does not endorse a first-handed understanding of the facts based on one's own evaluation of the evidence. She again insists that students accept what an authority tells them: "The Ministry of Magic guarantees that you are not in danger from any Dark wizard."

The second-handed approach of uncritically accepting the pronouncements of an authority brings with it one main problem: an authority can be wrong, manipulative, or vicious. Umbridge is perfectly willing to accept and promote Fudge's baseless and paranoid assertion that Harry and Dumbledore are lying about Voldemort's return. Then, after the Ministry accepts the facts about Voldemort, Umbridge bows to the authority of the new regime as easily as she did to the old.

Finally, when the Ministry of Magic falls to Voldemort's forces and Voldemort installs his own puppet minister, Umbridge remains loyal to the Ministry's authority. When Harry and his friends break into the Ministry's headquarters, Harry sees Umbridge and her new office. The plaques on the door read, "Dolores Umbridge: Senior Undersecretary to the Minister; Head of the Muggle-Born Registration Commission." Just as the Nazis registered and persecuted Jews, so the Ministry of Magic under Voldemort registers and persecutes "Muggle-born" wizards (those born of non-magical parents).

Harry finds Umbridge interrogating wizards thought to be Muggle-born. Just as Umbridge falsely accused Harry of lying about Voldemort, based on the ministry's authority, so Umbridge falsely accuses Muggle-born wizards of stealing their wands, based on the same authority. Moreover, just as Umbridge subjected Harry to physical abuse and even the risk of death, so Umbridge subjects her new victims to torture, imprisonment, and threat of destruction.

Umbridge's behavior reveals the connection between a second-handed acceptance of an authority and the use of authority to punish. Harry and his allies seek to persuade peaceable people through reason. They resort to force only when attacked, in self-defense. When one relies on reason—logical evaluation of the evidence—one counts on others' first-handed ability to follow the reasoned arguments and independently check the evidence. But one who expects others to take the word of an authority, without independent verification, must instead rely on deception, intimidation, or, ultimately, brute force. It is no surprise, then, that Umbridge simultaneously accepts an authority over her, expects others to believe whatever the authority tells them, and exerts authority over others in the form of physical force.

Next we turn to the example of Voldemort, the ultimate manifestation of evil in the Harry Potter books. While his evil extends far beyond the vice of second-handedness, he is the extreme example of the power-seeking second-hander.

On the surface, Voldemort seems quite different from Umbridge. He accepts no authority over him but seeks to impose himself as the authority. To his followers, "the Dark Lord's word is law."

Yet, like Umbridge, Voldemort uses force against others to get them to accept authority. Just after he regains power, he tries to put Harry under a controlling curse, which Harry resists. Voldemort says, "Harry, obedience is a virtue I need to teach you before you die. …Perhaps another little dose of pain?"

Umbridge and Voldemort are similar in their efforts to subject others to authority. Are they fundamentally different in that Umbridge accepts an authority over her, while Voldemort believes himself to be the ultimate authority? No. Voldemort, like Umbridge, bases his life on the beliefs and views of other people. In seeking power over others, Voldemort makes others the focus of his life. In this sense, he is a second-hander through and through, just like Umbridge.

By showing Harry old memories from various sources, Dumbledore reveals Voldemort's past. When Dumbledore first meets Voldemort, who as a youth goes by his given name of Tom Riddle, the young wizard expresses his satisfaction at being above other people and able to control them: "I can make bad things happen to people who annoy me. I can make them hurt if I want to. …I knew I was different. …I knew I was special."

Dumbledore notes that, even prior to any formal instruction, Riddle "was already using magic against other people, to frighten, to punish, to control"; he had "obvious instincts for cruelty, secrecy, and domination." Riddle dislikes his first name because "Tom" is too common. Dumbledore explains, "There he showed his contempt for anything that tied him to other people, anything that made him ordinary. Even then, he wished to be different, separate, notorious. …Tom Riddle was already highly self-sufficient, secretive, and, apparently, friendless." However, Riddle's "self-sufficiency" was not that of a first-hander, who reaches his own conclusions and achieves his own values. Instead, Riddle evaluated himself in comparison to others. He wanted to be different…from others. Separate from, but in control of, others. Notorious…in the eyes of others.

Dumbledore continues, "The young Tom Riddle liked to collect trophies. ...These were taken from victims of his bullying behavior, souvenirs, if you will, of particularly unpleasant bits of magic." Riddle stole objects from others in order to demonstrate (to himself) his superiority. Later, Riddle murders others to gain objects of importance from them. Dumbledore notes, "Voldemort had committed another murder...not for revenge, but for gain. He wanted...two fabulous trophies." One of those objects "had belonged to another of Hogwarts's founders." Voldemort likes to collect things, not by earning them but through force, and not because he enjoys their qualities directly but because they represent his superiority.

When Voldemort rises to power, he takes special delight in practicing the three Unforgivable Curses. Notably, each of these curses is about controlling others. The Imperius Curse enables one to control the movements and behavior of others. The Cruciatus Curse inflicts unbearable pain on the victim; prolonged exposure can result in insanity. And Avada Kedavra kills. These (and their counterparts in our world) are the ultimate weapons of the second-hander who seeks power.

When Voldemort overthrows the Ministry of Magic, he places within it a symbol of dominance—a statue showing "a witch and a wizard sitting on ornately carved thrones," structures composed of Muggles, "hundreds and hundreds of naked bodies, men, women, and children, all with rather stupid, ugly faces, twisted and pressed together to support the weight of the handsomely robed wizards."

Voldemort, however, does not merely wish to place wizards above Muggles; he wishes to place himself above all wizards. Voldemort sees Muggles as worthy of nothing but slavery to wizards, and he also condemns so-called Mudbloods and blood traitors. Though the statue represents wizards as superior to Muggles, even "pure blood" wizards are to be subjected to Voldemort's total authority.

Voldemort's entire motivation is to place himself in superiority over all others. His aspirations depend completely on his position relative to other people. In attempting to place himself in power over everyone else, Voldemort makes his entire life utterly dependent on everyone else. This is the exact opposite of a first-handed approach, which centers on one's own judgment and values, relates to others through reason, and judges one's value independently. Voldemort is therefore an archetype of this particular sort of second-hander.

Another type of second-hander wishes to follow a power figure. Even though Umbridge accepts a higher authority, both she and Voldemort mainly want to exercise power over others. Some, though, are motivated mainly by a desire to prostrate themselves before power. This is true of some of Voldemort's followers. Even though they gleefully harm and control others, they do this primarily to impress Voldemort. A sort of mirror image of the second-hander who seeks power, then, is the second-hander who seeks to be dominated, a relative of seekers of social status.

Barty Crouch, Jr., the wayward son of the Ministry official discussed previously, and Bellatrix Lestrange offer two examples.

Crouch, in disguise, manages to deliver Harry to Voldemort. Harry escapes, but Crouch captures him again and intends to kill him. Crouch eagerly anticipates Voldemort's reaction: "Imagine how he will reward me…I will be honored beyond all other Death Eaters. I will be his dearest, his closest supporter…closer than a son."

Bellatrix becomes incensed when Harry dares to speak the name of Voldemort and suggest (correctly) that Voldemort's father was a Muggle. She too imagines that she "was and [is] the Dark Lord's most loyal servant." Only a short time later, however, when she fails to successfully complete one of Voldemort's commands, she begs, "Master…do not punish me." For Voldemort, punishment usually means the torturing curse. Bellatrix's relationship with Voldemort is one of masochism and delusion. Even after she provokes Voldemort's anger, she continues to claim, "He calls me his most loyal, his most faithful." That does not prevent Voldemort from nearly killing her in a rage. Later, Bellatrix believes that Voldemort has struck Harry dead: "'My Lord…*my Lord*…' She spoke as if to a lover."

Yet, as Dumbledore explains to Harry, "You will hear many of his Death Eaters claiming that they are in his confidence, that they alone are close to him, even understand him. They are deluded. Lord Voldemort has never had a friend." The only thing that Bellatrix truly loves is subservience to a powerful figure.

The First-Handers

We have seen several forms of second-handedness, from the drive for unearned social standing to the quest for power over others to the wish to be controlled. The common trait of all second-handedness is living one's life according to the opinions, expectations, or position of others.

Now we turn to the first-handed heroes of the books, those who think for themselves and choose their own values—including honest and mutually respectful relationships with others—based on what they independently understand to be moral and good for their lives. While all of the heroes act first-handedly (at least most of the time), three characters offer especially clear examples of first-handed living: Dobby, Hermione, and Harry.

Dobby pushes the boundaries of the magic that binds him to slavery, then he embraces his freedom. Contrast Dobby's independence with the servility of Winky. When Winky's master, Barty Crouch, Sr., catches her in a position that embarrasses him, he punishes Winky by freeing her. She cannot imagine living a life of freedom—making her own choices, free of the imposed will of others. "No, master!" she begs.

Later we find Dobby and Winky working in the kitchens of Hogwarts. Dobby, against all tradition, wears strange clothing as a celebration of his freedom, for it is the gift of clothes that breaks the magical bonds of slavery. While Dobby relishes his freedom, Winky abhors hers. When Harry finds her in the kitchen, she has let her clothes become filthy, and she has taken to drink and perpetual sobbing.

Harry learns that Dobby has spent two years looking for a job. The elf explains, "But Dobby hasn't found work, sir, because

Dobby wants paying now!" The other house-elves "all looked away at these words, as though Dobby had said something rude and embarrassing." Unfortunately, Dobby finds, "most wizards don't want a house-elf who wants paying." Dobby defies the expectations of wizards and elves alike: "Dobby likes work, but he wants to wear clothes and he wants to be paid, Harry Potter. ...Dobby likes being free!" Finally, Dobby finds work for himself and for Winky when Dumbledore agrees to accept them at Hogwarts. However, Winky refuses payment; she says: "Winky is properly ashamed of being freed!" Dobby even delights in his ability to call Dumbledore "a barmy old codger," though he has far too much respect for the headmaster ever to do that. Dobby does not automatically do what he is told but what he understands is right and best for him.

Hermione too displays great independence. Against all the prejudices of the wizarding world, Hermione champions the cause of elfish rights. She realizes that elf slavery is wrong, and she fights it, regardless of tradition and social pressure. When Winky's master, Crouch, verbally abuses the elf, Hermione publicly upbraids him. Hermione challenges Percy Weasley, too; when he says that a "Ministry official...deserves unswerving obedience from his servants," Hermione cuts him off: "His *slave*, you mean!"

After spending hours in the library researching the issue, Hermione announces the formation of a new organization: S.P.E.W., or the Society for the Promotion of Elfish Welfare. Ron immediately mocks the acronym and retorts, "They *like* being enslaved!" Hermione ignores Ron and launches into a description of the aims of her organization. George Weasley, Ron's older brother and also a good friend, argues, "We've met [the elves of Hogwarts], and they're *happy*. They think they've got the best job in the world." Hermione replies, "That's because they're uneducated and brainwashed!" Hermione sticks to her principles even when hardly anyone supports her. She independently reaches her own conclusions, and then she acts on them, no matter what other people think or how they mock her.

Hermione also rejects the claims of authorities when she has grounds to doubt them. For example, when Hermione, Harry, and Ron find themselves in a Divinations class of dubious value, Hermione doesn't hide her contempt for the teacher, Professor Sybill Trelawney, even though several other students practically worship her. During one class, Trelawney pronounces, "The fates have informed me that your examination in June will concern the Orb." At that, "Hermione snorted," saying, "Well, honestly…'the fates have informed her'…who sets the exam? She does! What an amazing prediction!" A short time later, Trelawney claims to see an ominous omen in a crystal ball. Hermione is fed up. "Oh, for *goodness'* sake!…Not that ridiculous Grim *again*!" When Trelawney replies that Hermione seems not to have the alleged innate skill that Divinations requires, Hermione says, "Fine!…I give up! I'm leaving!" With that Hermione stalks out of the classroom, never to return.

When the horrible Professor Umbridge comes to the school, Hermione is more calculated in her rebellion. Hermione recognizes immediately the purpose of Umbridge's presence: "It means the Ministry's interfering at Hogwarts," she explains to Harry and Ron. During her first Defense Against the Dark Arts class, Umbridge commands the students to read a worthless section of a book. Hermione declines, even though "Harry could not remember Hermione ever neglecting to read when instructed to." Instead, she distracts the entire class by holding her hand in the air, even as Umbridge attempts to ignore her. Finally Umbridge relents. "Did you want to ask something about the chapter, dear?" Hermione: "Not about the chapter, no." Umbridge: "Well, we're reading just now…If you have other queries we can deal with them at the end of class." Hermione, undaunted, intentionally provokes Umbridge, continuing, "I've got a query about your course aims." Umbridge again attempts to exert her authority: "Well, Miss Granger, I think the course aims are perfectly clear if you read them through carefully." Hermione replies, "Well, I don't…There's nothing written up there about *using* defensive spells." This sets off the entire class.

In a subsequent class, Hermione continues her campaign of undermining Umbridge's authority. When Umbridge instructs the class to read the second chapter of the assigned book, Hermione raises her hand and says, "I've already read chapter two." Umbridge replies, "Well then, proceed to chapter three." Hermione: "I've read that too. I've read the whole book." Umbridge believes she can get the better of Hermione: "Well, then, you should be able to tell me what Slinkhard [the author] says about counterjinxes in chapter fifteen." Hermione does so, then adds, "But I disagree." Furthermore, Hermione offers a concise argument as to why Slinkhard is wrong. Umbridge replies, "Well, I'm afraid that it is Mr. Slinkhard's opinion, and not yours, that matters within this classroom, Miss Granger." Not only does Hermione express her own first-handed evaluation of the facts, but she self-consciously educates others in the class about Umbridge's authoritarian nature through a demonstration that the other students can in turn independently evaluate.

Finally, Hermione decides that the students need to learn defensive spells on their own. She cooks up a scheme to "learn Defense Against the Dark Arts ourselves," with Harry serving as the instructor. Hermione, Ron, and Harry put the word out to other students. When Umbridge bans student groups, the group defies her and meets in secret. At the first meeting, Hermione says, "I thought it would be good if we, well, took matters into our own hands."

As Umbridge becomes ever more controlling, the usually prim Hermione says with understatement, "D'you know...I think I'm feeling a bit...*rebellious*." This is not rebellion for rebellion's sake or to impress other superficially rebellious students: it is the rebellion of an independent thinker who knows the nature of her beliefs and values and why she holds them.

Before turning to Harry, we should look back to Hermione's first days at school to forestall a possible confusion about first-handedness. When Harry and Ron first meet Hermione, they do not like her. At one point, Ron says to Harry, "It's no wonder no one can stand her...she's a nightmare, honestly." Hermione rushes past them in tears. Harry tells Ron, "I think she heard you." Ron insensitively replies, "So? …She must've noticed she's got no friends." Hermione spends the rest of the day crying in the bathroom. Does this mean that Hermione is putting the opinions of others first? On the contrary, it means she realizes that, though her feelings are hurt, she needs to work on her social skills.

The first thing that Harry and Ron notice about Hermione is her "bossy sort of voice." Hermione immediately tells Ron that his attempted spell is "not very good, is it?" What prompts Ron's nasty comment is Hermione's undiplomatic correction of one of his spells; "You're saying it wrong," she snaps. Hermione tends to pay a lot of attention to other people's business, and she seems to go out of her way to be the teacher's pet. In small ways, then, Hermione sometimes acts like a second-hander.

Even though Ron is not courteous in his response, he makes Hermione realize that she is alienating some of the people whom she has a legitimate interest in earning as friends. Happily, the three finally make up when the boys save Hermione from an escaped troll. The spell that Ron uses to knock out the troll is the very one whose execution Hermione criticized. As Ron realizes the value of Hermione's bookishness, she recognizes his bravery and ability to act under stress. In gratitude, Hermione accepts the blame when a teacher yells at the three students for disobeying orders to go to the dorms. With this, Hermione realizes that pleasing the teachers does not always matter.

Hermione does care very much what Harry and Ron think, and that is because, by her own first-handed evaluation, Harry and Ron have earned her loyalty and expressed sensible opinions. Being a first-hander, then, is not the same thing as being a loner— far from it. A first-hander seeks friends based not on social status, deception, or intimidation, but based on real virtues in others that one recognizes and values independently.

Finally we consider the first-handedness of Harry. One of Harry's best qualities is his consistency in choosing his friends in a first-handed way. For example, when Harry first hears Draco Malfoy put down Hagrid, Harry replies, "I think he's brilliant."

Independence: Mark of the Hero

Likewise, when Harry meets Draco on the train, Draco makes fun of the Weasley family and tells Harry, "You'll soon find out some wizarding families are much better than others, Potter. You don't want to go making friends with the wrong sort. I can help you there." Harry replies, "I think I can tell who the wrong sort are for myself, thanks." Similarly, Harry maintains a friendship with Dobby, disregarding social pressure and wizarding traditions. Harry utterly rejects prejudices against so-called Mudbloods and blood traitors; those terms insult his two best friends (Hermione's parents are Muggles, while Ron's family is friendly toward Muggles). Harry also defends Lupin, despite social prejudices.

Harry is famous for his encounter with Voldemort, but he does not think his fame places him above others. Nor does he get carried away with attention. For example, while Harry's flying skills do bring him glory on occasion, he genuinely loves flying and playing Quidditch. While he loves showing up his competitive rivals, this is because a victory reflects skillful play. (He especially enjoys beating the Slytherins, most of whom he dislikes.) While some of his rivals resort to cheating, Harry plays the game to enjoy his own abilities. He does not play to make himself look good in the eyes of others or to cast superior airs.

Harry Potter and his friends show the nature and value of first-handed living. They think things through for themselves and resist pressure to conform to tradition or the popular view without good reason. They value people and things according to standards that they independently grasp and accept. The villains, on the other hand, see themselves primarily in relation to others and look to maintain their status, not advance their independent values. They seek social status or power over others through deception, intimidation, or force. The first-handers reject such means and deal with others by voluntary persuasion based on the facts.

I do not mean to suggest that Rowling's every line unequivocally endorses independence. For instance, in the final book Harry decides "simply to trust" Dumbledore with "no desire to doubt again." While he does this based on his first-handed evaluation of Dumbledore as a reliable authority, Rowling offers no clear distinction between this and dependent, blind acceptance. Despite an occasional ambiguous line, though, Rowling presents her heroes as fiercely independent in the sense explained.

The heroes live their lives the way that Rowling writes her books—by their own judgment. It is fitting that Rowling's novels have brought her global fame (as well as magnificent wealth) in the Muggle world comparable to Harry's fame in the wizarding world. Like Harry, Rowling realizes that the fame is merely incidental to the pursuit of fundamentally independent values; fame is a possible consequence, not a fundamental motivation. Part of the reason that much of the world loves Harry Potter is that Rowling would stand by Harry regardless of how many people hated him, as Harry stands by his friends regardless of what other people think. Harry Potter earns readers' first-handed respect, and so does J. K. Rowling.

We have now explored the nature of the heroic valuer and the need for the hero to think and act independently, in a first-handed way. Next we turn to the necessary prerequisite for the independent hero: free will. If people did not have freedom of will, they would become whatever their environment made them. Because people do have free will, they are able to choose whether to become a heroic valuer or to fall into villainy.

Chapter Three
Free Will: "It Matters Not What Someone Is Born"

THE HEROIC VALUER DESERVES praise for brave and virtuous deeds. The villain, meanwhile, deserves blame for misdeeds. Moreover, the hero treats others according to their character as shown in actions. The possibility of a hero, then, depends on the existence of free will, our ability to mold our own character and decide to do what is right versus what is wrong.

Absent free will, praise and blame seem pointless, as does our desire to make ourselves into heroes. If we are merely the product of our environment, if we cannot choose the course of our lives, then what good is it to want to do what is right?

J. K. Rowling solidly endorses free will. The heroes of the Potter books explicitly accept free will, and they also demonstrate it by making the right choices, regardless of upbringing and environment. That is not to say that everybody has the capacity of free will at every moment or acts in conditions that allow moral culpability. Free will has its limits, and Rowling explores these, too. Yet Harry and his allies show that a normal person in normal circumstances directs his or her own life, for good or for ill.

Rowling establishes a basic view of free will in her books. When Harry first arrives at school, the Sorting Hat sees in him various natural abilities, developed skills, and character traits: courage, intelligence, talent, and "a nice thirst to prove yourself." But this is not enough for the Sorting Hat to make a decision. Harry, having met Draco Malfoy and heard nothing but bad things about Slytherin from trusted friends, thinks to himself, *"Not Slytherin, not Slytherin."* The Hat presses Harry, but he doesn't budge. The Hat concludes, "Well, if you're sure—better be GRYFFINDOR!" Harry, then, chooses the path of virtuous bravery rather than the path of prejudice and mistreatment of others typical of Slytherins.

Yet Harry continues to wonder whether his Slytherin side will take over. Near the end of *Chamber of Secrets*, Voldemort, appearing as a younger version of himself through possession of a magical book, says to Harry, "There are strange likenesses between us…Both half-bloods [with one Muggle parent], orphans, raised by Muggles. Probably the only two Parselmouths [speakers of snake language] to come to Hogwarts since the great Slytherin himself. We even *look* something alike."

Later Dumbledore discusses these similarities with Harry. Dumbledore speculates that Voldemort "transferred some of his own powers" to Harry the night Voldemort tried to kill him. Then Dumbledore adds, "You happen to have many qualities Salazar Slytherin prized in his hand-picked students. His own very rare gift, Parseltongue—resourcefulness—determination—a certain disregard for rules…Yet the Sorting Hat placed you in Gryffindor. You know why that was. Think."

Harry replies, "It only put me in Gryffindor…because I asked not to go in Slytherin." To this Dumbledore replies, *"Exactly… Which makes you very different* from Tom Riddle. It is our choices, Harry, that show what we truly are, far more than our abilities."

While upbraiding Fudge, Dumbledore thunders, "You place too much importance…on the so-called purity of blood! You fail to recognize that it matters not what someone is born, but what they grow to be!" Soon thereafter, Dumbledore reminds his students that they have the power "to make a choice between what is right and what is easy." Clearly, then, Rowling takes the side of free will.

From Birth to Choice

Several examples from the books illustrate Dumbledore's claim that it doesn't matter what someone is born. One can be born to good or bad circumstances and choose to go in a good or bad direction, implying four basic combinations.

If free will did not exist, we would expect people born to good circumstances to turn out well. With free will, such people can choose for themselves a virtuous path. Ron and Hermione are both born to good, stable, loving families, and they both become great heroes of the stories. These cases, while admirable, do not take us very far toward understanding free will.

Various people apparently born to advantage, such as Dolores Umbridge and Peter Pettigrew, choose the wrong path. As we saw in Chapter Two, Percy Weasley goes against the rest of his family in search of social prestige. Some of the wealthiest families, such as the Malfoys, come to serve Voldemort. However, Rowling doesn't provide much background information on characters born to good circumstances who go bad. Families such as the Malfoys have long harbored ancient prejudices against Muggles, so such examples don't clearly illustrate free will.

The most interesting examples in the books, then, involve people born to bad circumstances who choose to be good, as contrasted with those who go from bad to worse. The three best examples of people who rise above their negative environments are Harry, Sirius, and Snape. (Dobby, an additional example, was discussed adequately in Chapters One and Two.) Before looking to those examples, though, we should look at the main example of someone who starts with lemons and brews a toxic stew.

That someone, of course, is Voldemort. While I've heard of childhoods more tragic than his, they are rare. We are introduced to Voldemort's family in *Half-Blood Prince*, when Dumbledore shows Harry captured memories. We first meet Voldemort's uncle, Morfin, a man missing several teeth who has nailed a snake to his front door. Morfin, who has attacked a Muggle, greets a Ministry official by attacking him as well. Then Voldemort's grandfather

Gaunt arrives on the scene, and he immediately equates "Muggles and filth."

Finally we meet Voldemort's mother-to-be, Merope. "Harry thought he had never seen a more defeated-looking person." Her father Gaunt calls her a "useless sack of muck," then nearly strangles her to show the Ministry official a necklace she is wearing that had belonged to Slytherin.

The Muggle that Morfin had attacked was Tom Riddle, Sr., Voldemort's father-to-be. When Morfin informs Gaunt of Merope's crush on Riddle, Gaunt lashes out in hatred: "My daughter—pure-blooded descendant of Salazar Slytherin—hankering after a filthy, dirty-veined Muggle?" Gaunt again tries to strangle his daughter but is stopped by the Ministry official.

When both Morfin and Gaunt are sentenced to Azkaban prison for their violence, Merope, "alone and free for the first time in her life," plotted "her escape from the desperate life she had led for eighteen years," Dumbledore tells Harry. With the handsome, wealthy Riddle well out of her league, and completely lacking the sense that accompanies a decent upbringing, Merope, desperately in love, gives Riddle a love potion. Dumbledore speculates that Merope, pregnant and sincerely in love with Riddle, stopped giving him the potion, at which time he left.

Later, Dumbledore reveals to Harry what an administrator of an orphanage said: "This girl...came staggering up the front steps. ...We took her in, and she had the baby within the hour. And she was dead in another hour." Voldemort, who grew up in the same orphanage until invited to Hogwarts, did not exactly live a life of advantage.

As we have seen, Voldemort mistreats others at the orphanage. Nevertheless, Dumbledore thought that Tom Riddle, Jr., might have "resolved to turn over a fresh leaf. I chose to give him that chance." Voldemort does not take it. Instead, he becomes progressively more rotten. After honing his cruelty at Hogwarts, Voldemort murders his father and grandparents and frames Morfin for the crime.

Was Dumbledore foolish to grant Voldemort a second chance, on the assumption that he could have turned his life around?

Or was Voldemort destined to turn out evil, given his tragic childhood?

The skeptics of free will hold that vile acts, while unfortunate, are not within the control of the perpetrators. While some such skeptics look to the influence of external circumstances, others look to internal conditions beyond conscious control. A classic example of this attitude is the defense of two real-life murderers, Nathan Leopold and Richard Loeb. Clarence Darrow, the defense attorney, argued in his closing statement:

> Why did they kill little Bobby Franks? Not for money, not for spite; not for hate. They killed him as they might kill a spider or a fly, for the experience. They killed him because they were made that way. Because somewhere in the infinite processes that go to the making up of the boy or the man something slipped…
>
> The emotions are the urge that make us live; the urge that makes us work or play, or move along the pathways of life. They are the instinctive things…The intellect does not count so much. …[T]he emotional life…comes from the nerves, the muscles, the endocrine glands, the vegetative system. …
>
> Is Dickey Loeb to blame because out of the infinite forces that conspired to form him, the infinite forces that were at work producing him ages before he was born, that because out of these infinite combinations he was born without [a normal emotional system]? …Is he to blame for what he did not have and never had? Is he to blame that his machine is imperfect? Who is to blame? I do not know. I have never in my life been interested so much in fixing blame as I have in relieving people from blame. I am not wise enough to fix it. I know that somewhere in the past that entered into him something missed. It may be defective nerves. It may be a defective heart or liver. It may be defective endocrine glands. I know it is something.[10]

Did some part of Voldemort beyond his conscious control just "slip," such that he became the worst mass-murderer in wizarding history? Or did he choose to make the worst out of a bad situation?

Rowling shows that choice is key. She does this primarily by showing characters of comparable backgrounds who make a conscious decision to go in a different direction. While the examples she offers are part of a fictitious story, they mirror real-life examples that demonstrate the possibility of choice.

As we saw in Chapter One, Harry grows up in a situation in which he is denied love, constantly berated and bullied, routinely locked beneath the stairs, and given barely adequate nutrition. Harry's circumstances as a child are at least as bad as Voldemort's at the orphanage. Yet, as we saw, Harry does not grow bitter over this and devote his life to spite and revenge; instead, he welcomes a better life filled with love and friendship. While Voldemort goes to Hogwarts to build a cult following and hone his powers for evil, Harry goes to Hogwarts to build his life, enjoy his friends, and learn the skills useful for a happy, productive future.

Growing up before Hogwarts, both Harry and Voldemort realize that they have unusual abilities. Yet only Voldemort takes his nascent magical powers as a sign that he is superior to those around him. And only Voldemort consciously uses his powers to control and harm others.

Harry and Voldemort react quite differently upon learning that they are wizards. Upon first meeting Harry, Hagrid says, "Harry—yer a wizard." Harry replies, "I'm a *what*?" Harry's jaw drops in wonderment. Harry "felt quite sure there had been a horrible mistake." With Hagrid's probing, Harry recalls that he had managed to mysteriously escape Dudley's gang, regrow his hair, and set loose a (harmless) snake on Dudley. Harry reacts in pleasant surprise and hopefulness. He does not dream of taking a nasty revenge on the Dursleys, nor of using his magic to assert power over others.

Voldemort's response is quite different. When Dumbledore first greets him, Riddle tries to magically control Dumbledore's mind (which obviously doesn't work). When Dumbledore affirms that Riddle can do magic, Riddle replies, "I can make things move without touching them. I can make animals do what I want them to do, without training them. I can make bad things happen to people who annoy me. I can make them hurt if I want to." He adds (as we saw in Chapter Two), "I knew I was different. ...I knew I was special." Voldemort's sense is one of superiority and glee in the possibility of improving his ability to "make bad things happen." It is true that Voldemort's reaction does not spring up from nowhere; it is rooted in a lifetime of anger, spite, and narcissism, while Harry's reaction is rooted in a lifetime of patient longing for a life filled with values.

Rowling, then, does not suggest that changing one's character and making the right choices is easy or automatic; instead, she shows that our choices tend to become habituated and shape our character over time. But what can be shaped can be reshaped, and old habits can give way to new. The choice is up to the individual.

Neither Harry nor Voldemort knows much about his parents before entering Hogwarts. Harry believes that his parents died in a car crash, while Voldemort knows that his mother died following labor. Harry does not know that his parents died trying to save him, and Voldemort does not know about his father or the extent of his mother's tragedy. Thus, parental circumstances play no role in the boys' difference of attitudes. In general, neither external circumstances nor defective glands can explain the differences between the paths of Harry and Voldemort. The two make different choices.

Our next example of someone who rises above his circumstances is Sirius Black. As a child, Sirius was, like Draco Malfoy, inculcated in the most horrid prejudices. When we first enter Sirius's house in *Order of the Phoenix*, we meet a talking portrait of Sirius's mother. She screams at the Order's members, "Filth! Scum! By-products of dirt and vileness! Half-breeds, mutants, freaks, begone from this place!" And to Sirius she says, "Blood traitor, abomination, shame of my flesh!"

Sirius chooses not to adopt the prejudices of his family. Instead, he becomes best friends in school with James Potter and Remus Lupin. Sirius tells Harry that he ran away from home at the age of sixteen and went to stay with the Potters.

Sirius says that he left "because I hated...my parents, with their pure-blood mania." His parents were not Death Eaters, but "they thought Voldemort had the right idea, they were all for the purification of the Wizarding race, getting rid of Muggle-borns and having purebloods in charge." Sirius doesn't suffer poverty as a child, as do Voldemort and Harry, but he is constantly subjected to the prejudices that drove many children of "pureblood" families first to Slytherin and then to the service of Voldemort. For example, Sirius's relatives Bellatrix Lestrange and Narcissa Malfoy become Death Eaters. What makes Sirius different? He assumes the responsibility of thinking for himself and choosing his own friends; doing so guides him to reject irrational prejudices and befriend virtuous people, whatever their background.

Professor Severus Snape, the next example, proves to be one of the greatest mysteries of the books. Harry immediately hates him and assumes he's up to no good. Near the end of *Half-Blood Prince*, Snape kills Dumbledore. It is not until the final book that we learn definitively that all along Snape was working as Dumbledore's spy to help bring down Voldemort.

We learn of Snape's heroism only after his murder at the hands of Voldemort, when Harry is able to view a collection of memories that Snape left for him. Snape is a shabbily dressed, socially awkward child. Snape befriends Lily Potter before they enter Hogwarts. Snape, realizing that Lily's parents are Muggles, resists the prejudices widespread among wizards. Lily asks him whether Muggle-birth matters; Snape answers, "No...It doesn't make any difference."

Snape, whose fighting parents create a troubled home life, struggles between his better and worse natures. When Petunia (Lily's sister) makes fun of him, Snape causes a branch to fall on her, angering Lily. Snape also tends to look down on Petunia, as she is a Muggle, though he fights this inclination, too. He feels jealous of the popular James and Sirius, who mock him. His friends tend to abuse people and finally join with Voldemort, alienating him from Lily. After taking some abuse from James, "in his humiliation and his fury" he calls Lily a Mudblood, which is comparable to a terrible racial epithet.

Finally Snape joins the Death Eaters. Snape gives Voldemort the prophesy which, Snape is horrified to learn, leads Voldemort to target the Potters. Finally Snape awakens from the horror of his behavior and warns Dumbledore. But he is too late. Voldemort strikes, killing Lily, the only person Snape ever loved.

This leads to one of the most heart-wrenching scenes in the series, one of the stories that elevates Rowling's books to the heights of great and enduring world literature. Dumbledore informs Snape that Lily's son lives. "He has her eyes, precisely her eyes. You remember the shape and color of Lily Evans's eyes, I am sure?" Snape pleads, "DON'T! …Gone…dead." Dumbledore queries, "Is this remorse, Severus?" He answers, "I wish…I wish *I* were dead." But Dumbledore tells him he must work against Voldemort and protect Harry. "If you loved Lily Evans, if you truly loved her, then your way forward is clear." From this point on, though Snape remains an embittered and often mean man, he never wavers from his loyalty to Dumbledore, even when Dumbledore asks Snape to kill him for his students and his cause.

Harry finds Snape just before he dies. Snape's final words to the son of his only true love, the son with his mother's eyes, are "Look…at…me."

It is a devastating story, and one that shows that choice is possible, that remorse is possible, that a reformation of one's character is possible. Snape chooses Lily's love over Voldemort's evil, and that is the only thing that gives the rest of his troubled life any meaning or value. After Harry and Ginny marry, Harry names his son Albus Severus, after Dumbledore and Snape, the two men in the novels who started down the wrong path and then chose to change course.

Remorse is the vehicle by which the wayward return to the values of life. Remorse is a theme with Snape and other characters as well. Dumbledore returns to the theme of remorse when, in spirit form, he talks with Harry at King's Cross. As we will explore in greater detail in Chapter Four, as a young man Dumbledore joins with Voldemort's precursor, Gellert Grindelwald, when Dumbledore dreams of "Muggles forced into subservience... wizards triumphant." Dumbledore later confesses, "Oh, I had a few scruples. I assuaged my conscience with empty words. It would all be for the greater good." Similar to the tragedy unleashed by Snape, Dumbledore's association with Grindelwald leads to the death of his sister. In discussing this, "Dumbledore gave a little gasp and began to cry in earnest." After mending his ways and coming to grips with his previous "arrogance and stupidity," Dumbledore defeats Grindelwald.

Unlike Voldemort, Grindelwald also awakens to his horrific past, though he is too late to salvage his life, as Dumbledore is able to do. When Voldemort visits Grindelwald in prison, the aged prisoner refuses to help him, so Voldemort kills him. Dumbledore tells Harry, "They say he showed remorse in later years, alone in his cell...I hope that it is true. I would like to think he did feel the horror and shame of what he had done."

The last time that Harry confronts Voldemort, Harry says, "I'd advise you to think about what you've done. ...Think, and try for some remorse, Riddle." While Harry does not expect such remorse, he thinks that it is possible, even though Voldemort has gone much too far down the path of evil ever to salvage any part of his life.

I'm not sure that it's possible for the great monsters of history ever to show remorse, for they have so deeply entrenched self-deception and irrational hatred that remorse may be beyond them. Yet clearly in cases like those of Snape and Dumbledore remorse is possible.

Remorse consists of thinking deeply about the nature of one's errors, feeling profound regret, and recommitting one's self to a life of values. For all except perhaps the most heinous crimes, remorse is possible, and it is necessary for a return to a life filled with values and joy.

The possibility of remorse further illustrates the presence and power of free will. Remorse is only necessary if one makes bad choices; Sirius begins with the right decisions and needs no remorse. One may, through remorse, choose to forsake the bad in favor of the good. Even though Voldemort never shows remorse and continuously takes himself further from that possibility, he had the chance for remorse when he was a student at Hogwarts. Dumbledore hoped that, as a new student, "it was possible that he felt sorry for how he had behaved before." It is possible—that is what our freedom of will enables, despite our circumstances, even if we've made mistakes in the past.

Limits of Free Will and Action

The fact that we have free will does not mean that we are free in every respect. Our will can be limited in particular ways, and surrounding circumstances can limit the options open to us. We'll look at several of the limits of free will and action that Rowling presents.

We must first distinguish between freedom of will and context of action. Free will involves the "power to control [one's] consciousness," to bring one's mind into focus, as philosopher Leonard Peikoff explains. What one can do with this freedom, however, depends upon one's background and prior decisions. Willing one's mind to come to full awareness does not mean that a person can exceed his or her capacities. Peikoff continues, "'Full awareness' does *not* mean omniscience. It means the awareness attainable by a man who seeks to understand some object by using to the full the evidence, the past knowledge, and the cognitive skills available to him at the time."[11]

Such knowledge and skills necessarily are limited both by external conditions and by one's prior choices. External conditions include education, historical discoveries of others, quality of parenting, and the like. As we make more choices, our knowledge and skills increasingly become the product of those choices. If one pays attention in study, critically examines the claims of others, tries hard to understand the facts, and so on, then one will expand one's knowledge and mental capacities.

We have free will whenever we are able to bring our minds into focus. A person lacks such ability when asleep or in a coma, for instance. But the context in which a person acts is limited by knowledge, mental capacity, and external circumstances. For example, if I bring my mind into focus and realize that I need to eat nutritious food to stay alive, yet I am chained to a wall, my ability to practice or engage my freedom of will is severely restricted. A discussion of free will must encompass not only the fundamental choice to focus but also the ability to act given one's circumstances.

One limitation of action is genetics. Some Muggles are born tall, and they are more likely to make better basketball players. Only women are capable of bearing children. Some people are born with certain diseases. Will alone cannot change such things. In Rowling's world, people are born with or without the ability to do magic, and nobody can alter that. Hermione is a witch, even though she is born of Muggle parents. Some children of magical parents are born without the ability to do magic (they are called Squibs). While giants have less intelligence, Hagrid, a half-giant, is born with a human mind and the ability to do magic. While Rowling never mentions the source of magical powers, they are an innate ability akin to a genetic trait.

Rowling hints that genetics may predispose people to certain characteristics. Dumbledore explains that the Gaunts, the family to which Merope belongs, are "noted for a vein of instability and violence that flourished through the generations due to their habit of marrying their own cousins." I am not convinced that genetics actually can predispose a person to violence. Whether and to what extent it is possible, though, clearly Rowling treats the Gaunts as culpable for their crimes, and after all the Gaunt line chose to intermarry for reasons of prejudice.

Even if one were predisposed to certain tendencies, one could still choose which tendencies to strengthen and which to weaken. While Merope controls Riddle, she does so from misplaced love;

she doesn't display the brute physical violence of her father and brother. Clearly predispositions are not fate; for example, people are predisposed to like sex but may still choose to remain celibate. Possible predispositions, then, do not limit action, though they may make certain choices more difficult. Presumably Voldemort with his Muggle father would not have inherited violent tendencies, anyway.

Another limitation of action is physical disability. Someone without arms is not destined to make a great baseball pitcher (though someday artificial or transplanted limbs might make it possible). Someone with brain damage may not be able to control certain behaviors. In Rowling's world, Ariana, Dumbledore's sister (whom we will meet again in Chapter Four), does not have the ability to control her magic, owing to severe childhood trauma. Remus Lupin cannot control the fact that he turns into a werewolf, though he can retain conscious control if he takes the right potion.

In addition to purely physical conditions, mental conditions also can limit possible actions. The first condition is youth. A newborn infant does not have the power of choice. An infant relaxes to a tender embrace, cries from hunger or physical discomfort, and does little else. As one grows up, one develops the ability to direct one's mind and use it in the context of one's acquired knowledge and mental capacities.

Freedom of action and moral culpability depend on the ability to reason. As we saw when discussing remorse, the wayward often are told, "Think about what you've done." An infant does not have the ability to reason; an adult does. This ability develops over time; there is no fine line dividing one state from the other. Though we acquire freedom of will early in childhood in the sense of being able to direct our attention and thoughts, a context of action that allows for moral blame and praise requires a certain amount of knowledge and experience.

Generally in the Muggle world we recognize lesser culpability for young people. Typically criminal offenders under the age of eighteen receive lighter punishments, while those even younger often get more leniency. Of course, eighteen is a somewhat arbitrary marker; some mature before then, while others (me included) take a bit longer. The age of adulthood is seventeen in Rowling's magical world. Regardless of specifics, though, generally we recognize that, as children mature to adulthood, they develop the ability to reason, make decisions, and control their lives.

Dumbledore, who himself fell into youthful errors, recognizes that the young don't always have a fully developed ability to think for themselves. That is one reason why Dumbledore is more forgiving of Draco's errant ways. When Harry is a child, Dumbledore takes special care to protect him from the potentially harmful influence of fame. When Professor McGonagall questions the placement of Harry with the Dursleys, she points out that Harry will be "famous—a legend…there will be books written about Harry—every child in our world will know his name!" Dumbledore replies, "Exactly…It would be enough to turn any boy's head. …Can't you see how much better off he'll be, growing up away from all that until he's ready to take it?" Dumbledore realizes that the young often are particularly susceptible to social conditions, and he realizes that early fame might negatively influence Harry. (Dumbledore doesn't realize that the Dursleys will treat Harry so miserably.) We needn't reject free will to recognize the crucial importance of good parenting and healthy influences.

Dudley Dursley offers a prime example of what happens to a boy when his parents spoil him. He throws tantrums to get his way, and his parents encourage the practice. The Dursleys encourage Dudley to mistreat Harry, and Vernon urges Dudley to poke people with a stick. As he grows into a bully, his parents offer him no correction or guidance. Dumbledore criticizes Vernon and Petunia for "the appalling damage [they] have inflicted upon" Dudley. It is not until the final book that Dudley starts to take control of his life and overcome his poor upbringing. He takes Harry's advice about hiding from Voldemort, despite his father's protestations. What's more, Dudley shows genuine concern for Harry—something his parents have never expressed—and thanks Harry for saving him from the dementors.

Even Harry's own father was a bit of a git growing up, as was his friend Sirius. James was a show-off, and he and Sirius pestered Snape relentlessly. The adult Sirius recounts to Harry, "We were sometimes arrogant little berks...Of course [James] was a bit of an idiot! ...We were all idiots! ...Look...your father was the best friend I ever had, and he was a good person. A lot of people are idiots at the age of fifteen. He grew out of it." Unlike Draco and Dudley, James never did anything seriously nasty, but he too took some time to fully get his wits about him.

Age, especially once one hits the teenage years, does not relieve one from moral responsibility. Older children have the ability to think through their decisions. (A good rule of thumb is that if you're mature enough to contemplate whether you have moral responsibility, you do.) Both Voldemort and Harry achieve the ability to think through their choices at a relatively young age. Nevertheless, we recognize that as people develop their ability to think independently, they gain a greater ability to control their own lives. Even juveniles have enough background knowledge to become morally culpable, yet we tend to give people a partial break, depending on how young they are, because they have not yet acquired much knowledge or fully developed their mental capacities.

If immature mental capacity partly limits the scope of possible action, diminished mental capacity does the same thing. As we've seen, Merope endures a horrible childhood, such that she never fully overcomes the trauma of her youth. We do not see Merope as an evil woman but as a victim of her vicious family. An even more striking example is Kreacher, the house-elf of the Black family.

Kreacher is severely abused and mistreated, and this reduces his moral culpability for betraying the Order of the Phoenix. Kreacher, bound by magic and tradition to the family he serves, works in a home that features the mounted heads of his dead ancestors adorning the walls. His masters are severely prejudiced against Muggles and wizards born of Muggles, and Kreacher picks up such attitudes. Sirius notes that the elf, who resents Sirius for leaving his mother, has "been alone too long...taking mad orders from my mother's portrait and talking to himself."

Kreacher lies to Harry, thereby helping Voldemort lure him into a trap. When Harry understandably erupts in anger, Dumbledore explains, "Kreacher is what he has been made by wizards…Yes, he is to be pitied. His existence has been as miserable as your friend Dobby's. …And whatever Kreacher's faults, it must be admitted that Sirius did nothing to make Kreacher's lot easier."

In *Deathly Hallows*, after Harry, Ron, and Hermione learn of Voldemort's past vicious treatment of Kreacher, the three realize that the elf had been most loyal to Sirius's brother Regulus, who showed him kindness. With Regulus dead, Kreacher's life is utterly lonely and miserable.

When Harry finally understands Kreacher's conditions and acts to improve them, Kreacher begins to transfer his loyalties to Harry. Both Harry and Kreacher come to realize that Regulus had turned against Voldemort in part for abusing the elf. Kreacher finally begins to help Harry. In the battle at Hogwarts, Kreacher leads the elves against Voldemort.

It is tempting to think that Rowling (through Dumbledore) is too easy on Kreacher. Yet we must imagine what it would be like to live in Kreacher's conditions. As a slave, his independence is forcibly and severely restrained. He has very little opportunity to acquire knowledge on his own or develop his reasoning skills. Kreacher is physically incapable of disobeying a direct order from his masters and is forced to torture himself if he even starts to disobey; such conditions are bound to create severe psychological trauma. He is hardly allowed any values of his own; the only bright spot in his life was Regulus. Such an existence is characterized by servility, radical dependency, fear, and pain. Once Harry restores to him some share of a decent existence, Kreacher slowly begins to develop the mental capacities to control his own life.

Dobby also suffers miserably under slavery, but not to the degree that his freedom of choice is completely undercut. We praise Dobby highly for his courage, but we pity Kreacher for his miserable conditions, which at least largely offset his culpability. In the end, Kreacher is able to choose whether to fight against Voldemort or to run, and he chooses to fight.

Free Will: "It Matters Not What Someone Is Born"

So far, we have considered limitations of action due to some internal immaturity, disability, or incapacity. In the case of Kreacher, a slave, and Merope, practically a slave, the incapacity is caused by enforced physical conditions. Narrower uses of physical force and the threat of force also can impede one's choices.

For example, after the crowded Quidditch World Cup, a group of Death Eaters causes mayhem and kidnaps several Muggles. "High above them, floating along in midair, four struggling figures were being contorted into grotesque shapes. It was as though the masked wizards on the ground were puppeteers."

The Unforgivable Curses control, hurt, or kill others; each subverts or destroys the choice of the victim, and these curses have direct counterparts in the Muggle world. Consider drugs used to facilitate rape, the Inquisition's torture devices, and daily homicides in big cities.

Other particularly magical forms of overpowering another's choice include love potions, which Merope used and to which Ron is subjected; truth potions; and the magical constraints of slavery. Dobby chooses to help Harry, but he cannot control the magical force that causes him to hurt himself for it.

The threat of force is also enough to limit both action and moral culpability. For example, Luna Lovegood's father, Xenophilius, goes from working against Voldemort to publishing propaganda in his favor, and he also tries to turn Harry over to Voldemort's forces. Why? "They took my Luna...Because of what I've been writing. They took my Luna and I don't know where she is, what they've done to her. But they might give her back to me." In this case, we don't blame Xenophilius for publishing material that Voldemort wants. If he doesn't, Voldemort's followers will murder Luna. (And, besides, any thoughtful wizard knows that Voldemort is censoring the press.)

We do, however, think badly of Xenophilius for trying to deliver Harry to Voldemort. While he does this in a foolish attempt to get back his daughter, and thus we don't loathe him for his motives, he should have told Harry what was going on and let him leave, which would not have further endangered his daughter. This is especially true given that he knows Voldemort is dishonest, Harry is a leader in the fight against Voldemort, and Luna is a loyal friend who would hate to see her father give Harry to Voldemort. Nevertheless, Xenophilius's ability to act on his own knowledge and values is limited. We don't blame him for publishing propaganda, and we only partly blame him for trying to turn over Harry.

The threat of force limits freedom of action but does not totally override free will the way that direct force does. Xenophilius's publishing options are severely limited by the threat of force. He would like to keep his daughter and himself safe and continue to publish information critical of Voldemort. He does not have that freedom. If he does not bend to Voldemort's commands, he risks losing his daughter and himself to murder. The threat of physical force undermines freedom of action to the extent of the severity of force threatened and the surety of it being carried out.

Excuses Don't Limit Freedom

We have seen a variety of ways in which capacity for action is limited, undermined, or utterly destroyed. At various instances, however, characters in the Harry Potter books invoke excuses that do not actually point to a limitation of free will or action.

We saw two such examples earlier. In *Prisoner of Azkaban*, Pettigrew claims that he was too frightened to resist Voldemort. Sirius is not fooled. It is true that Voldemort had made general threats of force, so Pettigrew, like everyone else, was in some danger. Yet Pettigrew actively sought to serve Voldemort even when he was in no immediate danger, even when doing so put all of his values at risk, and despite his numerous opportunities to subvert Voldemort's power. Pettigrew is a coward and a monster precisely because he retained free will and the capacity to act rightly, and he chose evil over good. The other example was Percy Weasley, whose ambition for power blinded him, but with a blindfold placed by his own hand.

Barty Crouch, Jr., offers another excuse for his service to Voldemort—spite toward his father. As we saw in Chapter Two,

Crouch hopes that he will become "closer than a son" to Voldemort. Crouch always felt that his own father "had never loved" him, so he sought a sort of revenge and substitute in the approval of Voldemort. Crouch's excuse is an instance of the popular refrain: "My childhood made me do it."

Crouch, as a grown man, however, has the capacity to deal with his childhood sorrows in a healthy way or in a vile, horrific way. He chooses the latter. Crouch was not physically abused as a child, so there is no way he could claim mental incapacity, nor was he even neglected, at least by his mother. Certainly his childhood was more pleasant than Harry's. Crouch chose to be a moral monster. The fact that he did so at least partly out of spite toward his father does not diminish his guilt, for he had free will, and he chose badly.

While excuses could be discussed endlessly, we will consider only one more: Quirrell's denial of morality. Quirrell, another of Voldemort's followers, tells Harry (as we've seen), "There is no good and evil, there is only power, and those too weak to seek it."

Quirrell's line reminded me of something that one of the Columbine High School murderers wrote: "My belief is that if I say something, it goes. I am the law, and if you don't like it, you die. If I don't like you or I don't like what you want me to do, you die."[12]

In the case of the book and of real life, the rejection of morality is not held as a serious view but as a pretext to faintly mask spite and irrational hatred. While we have not explored a positive moral theory, we have seen implicitly that moral behavior is necessary for the achievement of genuine, life-serving values. The claim that there is no morality is merely a pretense, a psychological cover for indulging vicious whims. In the cases of Quirrell and the Columbine murders, the villains lashed out at innocent people and ended up dead themselves. Certainly Harry does not take Quirrell's claim seriously, and neither should we. We hardly feel sorry for Quirrell when he falls prey to his own pretense. Quirrell's self-deceptive statement in no way limits his freedom of will or ability to act, so Quirrell is morally blameworthy for his despicable acts.

We have seen that the hero fights for values and does so through independent thinking and acting. This chapter explored a necessary precondition of the heroic valuer: free will. While certain conditions can limit or override the capacity for action, normally people have the ability to choose, to direct their own lives, and so they deserve praise for their heroism and blame for their misdeeds.

In the next two chapters we turn to issues of sacrifice and immortality. I'll argue that these two themes of Rowling's books clash with the theme of the heroic valuer but play a relatively minor role in the stories.

Chapter Four
The Clash of Love and Sacrifice

According to the Gospel of John, Jesus told his followers, "This is my commandment, that you love one another as I have loved you. Greater love has no man than this, that a man lay down his life for his friends."[13] Is this the true theme of J. K. Rowling's Harry Potter series?

In Chapter One, we considered three great acts of courage: Lily Potter giving her life to protect her son from Voldemort, Dumbledore giving his life to protect his students and his cause, and Harry willingly going to his death (or so he believes) so that his allies can finally defeat Voldemort. Are not these characters following the commandment and model of Christ?

Certainly Rowling's books include Christian themes. As we saw in the introduction, one Catholic sees in Rowling's books the themes of "love and self-giving." Dave Kopel writes that Rowling joins other fantasy writers such as J. R. R. Tolkien and C. S. Lewis in showing readers that "love and sacrifice…battle with death, at first appearing to be defeated, and then triumphing gloriously."[14]

John Granger, author of *Looking for God in Harry Potter*, argues that the Harry Potter books appeal to "the innate human hope that love conquers death and that we will rise from the dead in a resurrection made possible by and in Christ." This love, Granger adds, is a "*sacrificial* love."[15]

Yet I have suggested that the central theme of the Potter books is the heroic fight for values. What is the relationship between the theme of the heroic valuer and the theme of Christian love? To answer, we must untangle the concepts of love and sacrifice.

Love is a dominant theme of Rowling's books. Near the end of the first book, Dumbledore explains to Harry:

> Your mother died to save you. If there is one thing that Voldemort cannot understand, it is love. He didn't realize that love as powerful as your mother's for you leaves its own mark. ...To have been loved so deeply, even though the person who loved us is gone, will give us some protection forever.

The relationships of love well up from Rowling's books. Harry, Ron, and Hermione love each other as best friends. Later, Harry and Ginny develop romantic love, as do Ron and Hermione. Harry forms deep bonds of love with his godfather, Sirius Black, as well as with Dumbledore, Lupin, Hagrid, Dobby, and others. Harry's parents loved him dearly. The large Weasley family is bound tightly by love; even Percy, who abandons his family to advance his career with the Ministry of Magic, finally returns to a welcoming home as the Prodigal Son. Love is a central element of Rowling's stories and a central reason why readers love the books.

The relationship between love and the heroic fight for values should be evident. To love is to value. We value the people we love; love for other people is a particularly important manifestation of value. We can value other things as well, such as a good education, an interesting job, or a finely crafted broomstick or automobile. Often we say that we "love" such things. But love for other people is a crucial part of our lives, and our individual friends and loved ones are unique and irreplaceable. Primary among the values that the hero fights to defend are loved ones.

To better grasp the way in which loving people is a form of valuing, we can turn to Aristotle's views of friendship, found in the eighth and ninth books of *Nicomachean Ethics*. Aristotle writes:

[It is] most necessary with a view to living. For without friends no one would choose to live, though he had all other goods...for what is the use of such prosperity without the opportunity of beneficence, which is exercised chiefly and in its most laudable form towards friends? Or how can prosperity be guarded and preserved without friends? ...And in poverty and in other misfortunes men think friends are the only refuge...[W]ith friends men are more able both to think and to act.[16]

For Aristotle, then, friendship is a supreme value without which life is not worth living. He goes on to explain in greater detail why we need friends. Aristotle describes friendships of utility and pleasure, which are "only incidental; for it is not as being the man he is that the loved person is loved, but as providing some good or pleasure." These sorts of friendships abound in Rowling's books; for example, Harry buys goods from shopkeepers, plays sports with his Quidditch mates, and enjoys the services of bus drivers and restaurant owners. But Aristotle describes a third sort of friendship that is much more important.

"Perfect friendship," Aristotle writes, "is the friendship of men who are good, and alike in excellence..." This is the sort of friendship that Harry develops with Ron, Hermione, and Sirius. Even though Harry's relationships with Dumbledore and Lupin begin as ones of mentor and student, these relationships too develop into perfect friendships as Harry matures.

Aristotle describes perfect friendship in some detail; here we'll touch upon some of the highlights. "[T]hose who wish well to their friends for their sake are most truly friends..." "Further, such friendship requires time and familiarity...nor can [people] admit each other to friendship or be friends till each has been found lovable and been trusted by each."[17] "[T]he friendship of good men is good, being augmented by their companionship; and they are thought to become better too by their activities and by improving each other; for from each other they take the mould of the characteristics they approve..."[18]

The unique value of a perfect friend is that we are able to see virtue manifest in another person:

> [I]f we can contemplate our neighbours better than ourselves and their actions better than our own, and if the actions of virtuous men who are their friends are pleasant to good men…the blessed man will need friends of this sort, since he chooses to contemplate worthy actions and actions that are his own, and the actions of a good man who is his friend have both these qualities.

It is in this sense, Aristotle writes, that a "friend is another self."[19]

We have seen, then, that love is not only compatible with valuing but a necessary part of the heroic fight for values. What, then, is the role of sacrifice?

According to the Christian conception of love, the ultimate form of love is to sacrifice one's interests, and even one's very life, for the sake of others. By this view, Christ offered the greatest gift of love possible by allowing himself to be tortured and nailed to a cross so that people could be forgiven their sins. As another famous passage from the Gospel of John states, "For God so loved the world that he gave his only Son, that whoever believes in him should not perish but have eternal life."[20]

I do not doubt that Rowling intended a parallel between some events in her books and the Christian Passion. But how well does the parallel hold up? Let us take a second look at Lily's death.

Lily's death is, at best, superficially similar to Jesus's death. While God sent his son to die, Lily tried to save her son's life, and she would have preferred to save her own life as well as her son's by killing Voldemort first. While Jesus willingly died to save even the most despicable and evil people (on condition of their repentance), Lily risked her life in an attempt to save her own son from a particular aggressor. She did not give her life for strangers, the undeserving, or her enemies. Lily's goal was to protect the innocent, not to generate some sort of mystical force or institution through which others can be forgiven their sins through blood sacrifice. Finally, Lily had no idea that in dying she would give Harry some sort of magical protection. That magic is fortunate but unintentional. Rowling does not explain how this protection works other than to describe it as "ancient magic," so that magic must be taken as part of the imaginary background world, along with wands and spells.

Lily was not trying to sacrifice her life or any of her other values; she was instead trying to protect her highest value, her son. Thus, while Lily's actions clearly fit with the theme of the heroic fight for values, they do not fit well with the theme of sacrifice.

Part of the problem is the slippery and often-confused meaning of the term "sacrifice." The meaning of sacrifice is not merely to surrender any value. If it were, then trading a penny for a dollar would be a "sacrifice." Sacrifice in the moral sense is to give up one's "greater value for the sake of a lesser one or of a nonvalue," in the words of novelist-philosopher Ayn Rand.[21] By this meaning, sacrifice is the opposite of achieving real, life-sustaining values, including friendships and other constructive relationships. For Lily, the true sacrifice would have been to abandon her son to Voldemort's terror.

According to the Christian tradition, one who sacrifices for others is "selfless," a term that Rowling uses approvingly, while one who doesn't sacrifice for others is "selfish," without love or consideration for others. However, once we realize that one's values, including one's friends, are of critical importance to one's own life, then there is no conflict between the good of one's self and the good of one's friends and allies. Nor is there any need for any sacrifice of values. While one might have to surrender a lesser value for the sake of a greater one—for instance, one's safety for the life of a friend—such an action is not a sacrifice by Rand's understanding.

We can make a stronger point. Not only does the heroic valuer have no need for sacrifice, but the heroic valuer holds sacrifice—in the sense of giving up a greater value for a lesser one—as a grave evil. Sacrifice should be avoided, by this view. Of course, it is essential that the heroic valuer distinguish between whims and real values. For example, as we saw in Chapter One, while Peter Pettigrew claimed to follow Voldemort for his personal gain, obviously Pettigrew forsook and destroyed his authentic, legitimate, life-serving values.

Aristotle argues that a higher form of self-interest recognizes that the good of one's friends is good for one's self. We love our friends "for their sake," because they are good, Aristotle points out. He adds, "And in loving a friend men love what is good for themselves; for the good man in becoming a friend becomes a good to his friend. Each, then, both loves what is good for himself, and makes an equal return in goodwill and in pleasantness…"[22]

Aristotle directly tackles the matter of "whether a man should love himself most, or some one else." Aristotle describes a standard account of his day, which is similar to the Christian view:

> People criticize those who love themselves most, and call them self-lovers, using this as an epithet of disgrace, and a bad man seems to do everything for his own sake, and the more so the more wicked he is…while the good man acts for honour's sake, and the more so the better he is, and acts for his friend's sake, and sacrifices his own interest.

In this negative or debased form of self-love, Aristotle continues, people "assign to themselves the greater share of wealth, honours, and bodily pleasures." In debased self-love, people attempt to "gratify their appetites and in general their feelings and the irrational element of the soul." In other words, the debased form of self-love is driven by whim; it describes the way that Voldemort's followers tend to act.

However, Aristotle points out, there is a higher, rational, and noble form of self-love. Today the more common term for this is rational self-interest. The rationally self-interested person acts, in Aristotle's words, "justly, temperately," so as to "secure for himself the honourable course." This sort of "man would seem more than the other a lover of self." Aristotle concludes, "Therefore the good man should be a lover of self (for he will both himself profit by doing noble acts, and will benefit his fellows), but the wicked man should not; for he will hurt both himself and his neighbours, following as he does evil passions." Aristotle's description aptly distinguishes between the motives of Harry Potter's group and the followers of Voldemort.

Aristotle even directly addresses the case of the heroic valuer who risks his or her life. "It is true of the good man too," Aristotle writes, "that he does many acts for the sake of his friends and his country, and if necessary dies for them..." Such a person favors the "intense pleasure," the "noble life," and "one great and noble action" to "mild enjoyment," a "humdrum existence," and "many trivial" acts. One who achieves nobility by helping his true friends "is therefore assigning the greater good to himself."[23]

But is Aristotle opening the concept of nobility so wide that it could include Christ's sacrifice on the cross? No. He writes, "Men seek to return either evil for evil...or good for good..."[24] The view of Jesus is quite different. According to the Gospel of Matthew, Jesus said, "Do not resist one who is evil. But if any one strikes you on the right cheek, turn to him the other also...I say to you, Love your enemies..."[25] Jesus died on a cross out of love for his enemies.

Aristotle's view is more consistent with the behavior of the protagonists in Harry Potter. For example, when Bellatrix Lestrange nearly kills Ginny, Molly Weasley's daughter, Molly returns evil for evil. She does not love Bellatrix; instead, she screams, "Not my daughter, you bitch!" Then "Molly's curse soared beneath Bellatrix's outstretched arm and hit her squarely in the chest, directly over her heart," killing her.[26]

Aristotle's account lends credence to the view that Lily, Dumbledore, and Harry heroically defend their own values, even when that means risking their lives. These heroes struggle to defend the values that give their own lives meaning, and they refuse to sacrifice one of their higher values for a lesser one or for a nonvalue.

Additional cases further illustrate the point.

In the first book, Ron mentions sacrifice. Earlier we reviewed Harry's motives for struggling to stop Voldemort from obtaining the Philosopher's Stone. Harry wants to stop Voldemort from killing him and his friends and destroying the peaceable world in which Harry thrives. Ron and Hermione join him on this dangerous quest for similar reasons. When the friends must play as chess pieces to get past a giant chess board blocking the way to the Stone, Ron decides that he must be taken in order to let the others through. As a consequence, a chess piece knocks Ron out and drags him away, incapacitating him for the rest of the mission. Before he goes down, Ron tells the others, "You've got to make some sacrifices!" But this is not really a sacrifice in the sense of giving up a greater value for a lesser one; Ron accepts some risk and pain in order to save his most precious values, including his own family and future, from Voldemort. This isn't a true sacrifice at all—Ron is seeking to save everything that matters to his life.

Next, Dumbledore's friend Nicolas Flamel has the only Philosopher's Stone in existence, enabling him to live past the age of 665 years. When Harry finally captures the Stone, Dumbledore and Flamel agree to destroy it. "But that means he and his wife will die, won't they?" Harry asks. Dumbledore confirms that, after putting their "affairs in order…yes, they will die." However, Dumbledore suggests, the Flamels have grown weary with their extremely old age. Moreover, the Flamels recognize that, had the Stone survived, Voldemort would have tried to steal it again, keeping their lives in perpetual danger and threatening all their other values.

Near the end of the last book, Harry is able to talk to Lupin, who has died. Lupin says to Harry, "I am sorry…I will never know [my son]…but he will know why I died and I hope he will understand. I was trying to make a world in which he could live a happier life." Lupin regrets leaving his son, yet he recognizes that he fought to preserve his life's values, including his son's well-being and happiness.

It would push matters too far to claim that Rowling consistently portrays rationally self-interested heroes who refuse to sacrifice their higher values. At times, the actions of Rowling's heroes follow the Christian ideal of self-sacrifice. However, Rowling seems to have trouble entirely committing herself to sacrifice as a moral ideal.

Two Mixed Cases

Generally, Rowling's heroes act to protect and promote their own life-serving values, while Rowling's villains sacrifice and destroy the values necessary for life and happiness. In the two cases that we will consider, the motivations of Rowling's protagonists are ambiguous or sacrificial.

The first case occurs near the end of the last book. Harry, Ron, and Hermione seek an object that contains a piece of Voldemort's soul, as all such objects must be destroyed before Voldemort can be killed. Harry realizes that the object, a tiara or diadem, is in a huge, magical room at Hogwarts that contains enormous piles of treasures and junk accumulated over centuries. Just as the three friends see the diadem, Draco appears with his two thuggish sidekicks, Crabbe and Goyle, to capture Harry and turn him and the diadem over to Voldemort.

Of the three villains, Crabbe is the most reckless and evil. He first tries to knock over a large stack of junk, which would have harmed Ron and buried the diadem. Crabbe also tries to use a torturing curse on Harry and a killing curse on Ron and Hermione. Draco tries vainly to restrain Crabbe. Finally, Crabbe unleashes a magical fire that quickly consumes the room.

Harry, Ron, and Hermione manage to find two flying broomsticks, but before they can escape the room, "Harry heard a thin, piteous human scream from amidst the terrible commotion." Harry sees Draco and Goyle and dives to save them. Ron follows but yells, "If we die for them, I'll kill you, Harry!" Harry escapes the fire with Draco, while Ron and Hermione save Goyle. Crabbe is lost in the flames.

Harry's act in this case contains an element of self-sacrifice; he puts himself and his friends in danger in order to save enemies seeking to kill him. On the face of it, the rationally self-interested move would have been to escape the danger and leave the villains to suffer the consequences of their own vile acts.

However, Harry's motives in this case are mixed. Harry does have some legitimate personal interest in rescuing Draco—Harry realizes that Draco is not fully committed to Voldemort. In *Half-Blood Prince*, Draco plots to murder Dumbledore, yet his motive is to stop Voldemort from punishing his parents and him as well. Draco fears for his life and thus acts partly from fear of Voldemort's retaliation. Hidden, Harry witnesses Draco's final confrontation with Dumbledore, and Draco is unable to finish his task. Draco repeats to Dumbledore, "I'm about to kill you." Dumbledore replies, "My dear boy, let us have no more pretense about that. If you were going to kill me, you would have done it when you first disarmed me."

Later, Harry sees (by looking into Voldemort's mind) other ways that Voldemort coerces Draco. Voldemort forces Draco to torture another of Voldemort's servants. "Do it, or feel my wrath yourself!" Voldemort commands. Harry can see "Malfoy's gaunt, petrified face." Insofar as Voldemort forces Draco's actions, Draco remains free from moral blame. Even in the confrontation over the diadem, Harry realizes that part of Draco's motivation is fear of Voldemort's wrath. Harry therefore sees Draco as partly innocent and to that degree worth protecting.

Prior to the encounter involving the diadem, Draco also tries to help Harry, even if in a small way. When Voldemort's forces capture a disfigured Harry, Draco twice defies his own father by refusing to identify Harry. Harry can see that "Draco's expression was full of reluctance, even fear."[27]

Harry probably also sees Draco as less culpable because of the horrid prejudices instilled in him by his parents and because of his young age; Harry knows that even Dumbledore got off on the wrong track for a time when he was Harry's age (as discussed later). Apparently, Draco grows up to be a better man.

Nevertheless, Draco is at least partly responsible for his own actions, and he goes out of his way to interfere with Harry's quest for the diadem. Harry chooses to rescue not only Draco but also Goyle, who is clearly on Voldemort's side (if not as evil as Crabbe). Rowling mixes motives of self-interest with those of self-sacrifice.

Rowling also introduces a number of literary coincidences that align the act of saving Draco with Harry's own interests, as though Rowling cannot bring herself to fully commit to an act of self-sacrifice. Harry's purpose for being in the room is to recover the diadem so that he can destroy it, and Harry happens to achieve this end by swooping down to grab Draco to rescue him. When Crabbe starts the fire, Harry has not yet found the diadem. Harry realizes that Draco and Goyle are also after the diadem, so the rescue attempt increases Harry's chances of finding it with or near one of those villains. (Harry increases his chances of finding the diadem merely by flying around the room.) As it happens, neither Draco nor Goyle has the diadem, but Harry incidentally finds it after reaching Draco. Here Rowling—in effect if not in intent—introduces a lucky coincidence through which Harry accomplishes his own ends because of a self-sacrificial act.

Were Rowling completely committed to self-sacrifice as a moral principle, she could have written the scene differently. Rather than let Crabbe, the most evil of the three villains, become separated from the other two to die in the flames, Rowling could have had Harry rescue Crabbe as well. Instead of letting Harry find the diadem by luck after rescuing Draco, she could have had Harry find the diadem first and then still choose to save the villains. Finally, Rowling lets Harry discover that the diadem has been damaged by the flames only after he escapes the conflagration. Once the friends are safe, the diadem disintegrates, and Hermione realizes that the flame destroyed it. Rowling could have let Harry see the diadem disintegrate in the room, before he rescues the villains.

Another coincidence related to Harry's rescue of Draco appears shortly after the scene. Even though Harry could not know it at the time, saving Draco's life would indirectly help Harry defeat Voldemort. After Voldemort believes that he has killed Harry, he sends Draco's mother, Narcissa, to verify Harry's death. At this point, Narcissa doesn't care anything about Voldemort's plans; she only wants to see that her son is safe. She whispers to Harry, "Is Draco alive? Is he in the castle?" Harry whispers that he is. Then Narcissa lies to Voldemort about Harry: "He is dead!" This keeps Harry safe until he is able to rejoin the fight.

This meeting with Narcissa is another coincidence that aligns Harry's act of self-sacrifice in rescuing Draco with Harry's own interests. Yet in this case the events are not entirely coincidental; a hero who courageously saves another person's life often inspires others to help the hero in turn.

The fact that Rowling introduces these lucky coincidences indicates that her premises are mixed. She has Harry perform a self-sacrificial act, but she renders the act to be in his favor. Rowling seems to accept the widespread notion that sacrifice of higher values somehow leads to rewards.[28]

A second case that could be construed as self-sacrifice on the part of a hero is the youthful Dumbledore delaying his career to look after his troubled sister. Dumbledore suffered a tragic family history. When Dumbledore was a child, a group of non-magical boys brutally beat his six-year-old sister, Ariana, for doing magic. Dumbledore's brother explains:

> It destroyed her, what they did: She was never right again. She wouldn't use magic, but she couldn't get rid of it; it turned inward and drove her mad, it exploded out of her when she couldn't control it, and at times she was strange and dangerous. But mostly she was sweet and scared and harmless.

Dumbledore's father goes after the boys responsible, and for that he is sentenced to Azkaban prison, where he dies. The family keeps the attack secret, "because if the Ministry had known what Ariana had become, she'd have been locked up in St. Mungo's [Hospital for Magical Maladies and Injuries] for good." Unfortunately, a few years later Ariana accidentally kills her mother with her uncontrollable magic, leaving the three children without parents. Dumbledore, a gifted student ready to leave school, puts his career on hold to care for his siblings.

Dumbledore describes his reaction to the situation:

> I resented it, Harry…I was gifted, I was brilliant. I wanted to escape. I wanted to shine. I wanted glory. Do not

misunderstand me...I loved them. I loved my parents, I loved my brother and my sister, but I was selfish, Harry, more selfish than you, who are a remarkably selfless person, could possibly imagine.

So that, when my mother died, and I was left the responsibility of a damaged sister and a wayward brother, I returned to my village in anger and bitterness. Trapped and wasted, I thought!

Here Dumbledore, Harry's hero and mentor, explicitly endorses selflessness and proclaims selfishness a moral fault. However, Rowling again mixes elements of self-interest with self-sacrifice.

Dumbledore truly loves his sister; she is one of his dear values. Rowling's language (through Dumbledore) of selfishness and selflessness fails to convey the full moral significance of the event. According to the traditional account of morality that Rowling invokes here, selfishness means not caring about anyone, while selflessness means caring for loved ones. However, we have seen that Harry Potter and his friends often pursue their own self-interests *by way of* caring for their loved ones, who are critically important to their lives and happiness. Dumbledore chooses to care for the people *he personally loves*. He does not, for instance, abandon his sister so that he can care for a complete stranger.

Dumbledore's choices seem artificially constrained. For example, his brother suggests that St. Mungo's would have been bad for Ariana. Up until this point, readers have come to know St. Mungo's as a caring facility with competent staff. For example, Neville's parents are hospitalized there, and Harry sees Neville visiting them. Harry also visits Arthur Weasley, Ron's father, in the hospital after Arthur becomes injured. Perhaps during Dumbledore's youth the hospital was worse.

Oddly, Dumbledore sees his choice as binary: either care for his sister or pursue a career. Even if he had discovered a valid reason to keep Ariana out of St. Mungo's, Dumbledore, the cleverest person in the books, could have figured out some way to ensure good care of his sister while making room for his career.

The issue, though, is more complicated for Dumbledore than an apparent conflict between two of his values, his sister and his career. The youthful Dumbledore probably realizes at some level that his motivation in pursuing a career is impure. When he says, "I wanted glory," he does not mean merely that he wanted to be successful. He wanted control and power over others. Not long after his mother dies, Dumbledore falls in with the young, dark wizard Grindelwald, who is soon to become Voldemort's precursor. At the time Dumbledore writes "about Wizard dominance being for the Muggles' own good." He claims that magical "power gives us the right to rule, but it also gives us responsibilities over the ruled." With Grindelwald, Dumbledore seeks a "weapon that would lead us to power." While this happens after Dumbledore decides to care for his sister, the incident reveals a preexisting flaw in his character with which he had probably struggled for years.

In this light, Dumbledore's choice is quite different—it is between caring for a sister he loves and pursuing a career for the wrong reasons. By taking a step back in his career and holding on to his core values, eventually Dumbledore is able to identify and correct his misguided thinking and find his true calling, teaching at Hogwarts. Dumbledore finds much greater personal satisfaction with the career he chooses than he ever would have found seeking the "glory" of power. If Dumbledore had forsaken his sister, he would have sacrificed that genuine value for the sake of a nonvalue, a life-damaging career. Though Dumbledore resents his choice at the time, it shows that part of him pulled back from seeking power over others.

Dumbledore certainly does not overcome his lust for power at the moment he decides to care for his sister. Dumbledore then meets Grindelwald and falls into trouble with him. When Dumbledore's brother criticizes Grindelwald, the dark wizard responds with a torturing curse, finally shocking Dumbledore to his senses. As Dumbledore defends his brother, the three start a fight that ends up killing Ariana. Yet it is Dumbledore's prior commitment to caring for his siblings, however muddled that commitment, that enables Dumbledore to overcome the influence of Grindelwald. True, had Dumbledore chosen his career for the wrong reasons and sacrificed his sister, he might not have met Grindelwald when he did, but he would have destroyed his own character and left himself open to falling into greater temptation in his future.

Dumbledore's youthful problem is not that he "selfishly" lusts after a career of glory and power. His problem is that he fails to fully understand why protecting his siblings, whom he loves, is in his own self-interest and why pursuing power over others threatens to undermine and destroy his life-serving values.

In Chapter One, we saw that Rowling's heroes fight courageously for the values that give their lives meaning. In this chapter, I have argued that the heroic valuers act mostly from rational self-interest, not from selfless sacrifice. Even when Rowling introduces elements of self-sacrifice, they are muted and mixed with self-interest.

The theme of selfless sacrifice is not the only Christian element in the Harry Potter books; Rowling also makes clear that she believes in spiritual life after physical death. While Dumbledore and other heroes deal with death by looking to the afterlife, Voldemort clings to his physical body at all costs, which turns him into a vicious monster. We explore these issues in the coming pages.

Chapter Five
Materialism and Immortality

WE HAVE CONTRASTED THE theme of the heroic valuer with the Christian theme of self-sacrifice. Now we turn to another element of Christianity within J. K. Rowling's books: a belief in the immortal soul. While the heroes share such a belief, Voldemort does not. A major motivation of Voldemort is his pathological fear of death, which accompanies his obsession with physical objects and his treatment of other people as though they too were merely objects. How do these elements tie together within the Harry Potter books?

Before turning to Rowling's treatment of death and the physical body, we need to take another look at how the characters relate to physical objects and other people, for these things are connected.

Recall the Dursleys' attitude toward objects. When Dudley throws a tantrum over getting only thirty-seven presents for his birthday, his parents promise him still more. While the Dursleys give Dudley a second bedroom to store all the objects that he proceeds to destroy, they force Harry to sleep beneath the stairs and give him as little as possible. Vernon and Petunia treat objects as a means for showing affection for and favoritism toward their son—and for withholding the same from Harry. Dudley treats the objects as symbols of his superiority over Harry (a theme explored in Chapter Two). The Dursleys treat material objects not as things that add real value to life, but as symbols of social status and social expectations (recall Vernon's company car displayed for all the neighbors to see). Rather than seek out things that actually enhance their lives, they attempt to derive meaning from the mere possession of objects.

The same is true for other miscreants of the stories. When Harry first meets Draco Malfoy (whose last name translates as "bad faith"), Draco brags about his possessions.

For the characters, an unhealthy obsession with physical objects accompanies the treatment of others as though they were merely objects. The Dursleys think of Harry as a slug, and Draco sees Hagrid as a servant.

Like the Dursleys, Draco uses objects to put others in their place—generally beneath him. In Draco's first major confrontation with Harry, Draco takes one of Neville Longbottom's misplaced possessions after Neville crashes his broom and heads to the hospital wing. Draco intends to hide the item. For Draco, objects are a means for showing or exerting power over others.

The villains' attitude toward objects and people is a form of second-handedness, as discussed in Chapter Two. The villains see objects not as things that actually enhance their lives, but as means to gauge one's relationship with others. If Dudley and Draco have more things than others, or seize control of the possessions of others, they feel that they're better than others.

Contrast the attitude of the Dursleys and of Draco toward objects with the attitude of Harry and his friends. The heroes do not disdain physical objects; they appreciate them very much as means to enhance their lives. But the heroes do not gauge their value by objects or try to dominate others through the possession or use of objects.

When Hagrid delivers the invitation to Hogwarts, for example, he gives Harry a "squashed box" containing a "large, sticky chocolate cake with *Happy Birthday Harry* written on it in green icing." This object, which Harry opens "with trembling fingers," is a show of affection and friendly consideration.

Harry inherits "mounds of gold coins" from his parents, yet he does not let his wealth go to his head. Harry initially considers buying a "solid gold cauldron," but Hagrid easily talks him into sticking with pewter. Harry also buys schoolbooks, scales, and a telescope. Hagrid gives Harry an owl, which is "dead useful, carry yer mail an' everythin'." (The owl as a pet is a companion, not an inanimate object.) All these things are obviously useful for Harry's life at school. Harry's grandest purchase is his wand, an object that bestows great potential power.

Harry also appreciates the objects associated with the game of Quidditch. When an accident injures Harry and destroys his Nimbus Two Thousand flying broom, he laments the loss and refuses to allow a nurse to "throw away the shattered remnants" of the broom. "He knew he was being stupid, knew that the Nimbus was beyond repair, but Harry couldn't help it; he felt as though he'd lost one of his best friends."

For Rowling, material objects are not inherently good or bad; their value depends on why and how we acquire and use them. It's bad to use objects to subordinate or control others; it's good to use objects to enhance one's life.

Unlike Draco, Harry does not view possessions as signs of social superiority. For example, the Weasley family, beloved by Harry, is not wealthy. When Ron complains about getting hand-me-downs, Harry does not mock him for this or brag about his own wealth. Instead, Harry sympathizes by describing how the Dursleys gave him nothing but hand-me-downs from Dudley. Harry realizes that the Weasleys are good people with tight family bonds. Molly and her husband Arthur are loving and responsible parents who make sure that their children always have the essentials. Harry likewise forms a deep friendship with Remus Lupin despite his poverty.

Wealth and class do not grant status in Harry's eyes. Harry appreciates his friends for who they are, for their moral character and passions, because they bring joy and meaning to his life. In sharp contrast to the Dursleys and Draco, Harry cares nothing about social status or other attributes unrelated to character. He does not care whether people are rich or poor, unless their wealth or poverty reflects some moral flaw or virtue. Harry instead builds loving relationships with people of worthy character.

Materialism and the Pathological Fear of Death

Harry is a person of the world in the best sense of the phrase. He loves his friends, values his possessions, enjoys flying and playing Quidditch, and relishes his life at Hogwarts and in the broader magical world. Yet, though he loves the earth and the things of the earth, he is hardly a materialist in the crass sense of the term.

Materialism is one of those terms that carries many meanings. If materialism means simply an appreciation for the physical world and a healthy interest in life-enhancing material goods, then materialism is good. But here I use the term in its crass sense, to mean, as the *Random House* dictionary puts it, an "emphasis on material objects... with a disinterest in or rejection of spiritual values." If we take spiritual values in the broadest sense, not to imply a supernatural realm but to refer to consciousness and the values of our rational human nature, such as love, friendship, and virtue, then a crass materialism that rejects such values obviously is bad.

Crass materialism ties together an unhealthy obsession with physical objects and the treatment of others as mere objects. Without a healthy integration of mind and body, consciousness and the physical, one cannot relate physical objects to the values of the mind. If one fails to recognize spiritual values pertaining to consciousness, then the perfect friendship that Aristotle describes is impossible. Instead, the crass materialist views others as tools, stepping stones, or roadblocks to be used, squashed, or blasted out of the way.

If Harry and his friends show a healthy relationship with objects and people that takes seriously the values of consciousness, then Voldemort and his followers represent the height of crass materialism. In a banal form, the Dursleys and Draco mistreat others and see objects as status symbols. Voldemort takes these failings to their ultimate ends, using objects and sacrificing others to enhance his power.

As we saw in Chapter Two, even as a child Voldemort uses magic to hurt and control others, and he has no friends. Furthermore, he likes to collect trophies. "Bear in mind this magpie-like tendency,"

Dumbledore suggests. Eventually Voldemort kills to obtain his trophies. Rowling again clearly links domination of others with a tendency to see objects as symbols of status.

With the Horcrux, Voldemort adds a new element of crass materialism. A Horcrux represents the union of an obsession with objects, the domination of others, and a third evil: the pathological fear of death. How does this third element fit with the other two? If one obsesses over objects and treats people as objects, one will come to see one's self as an object, too, detached from values of consciousness. One will also come to obsess over one's physical body, despite the consequences to one's consciousness. To begin to delve more deeply into this idea, we should explore the Horcrux in greater detail.

The nature of a Horcrux is explained to Voldemort by one of his professors. Harry is able to capture the memory from that professor and view it with Dumbledore:

> A Horcrux is the word used for an object in which a person has concealed part of their soul. …You split your soul…and hide part of it in an object outside the body. Then, even if one's body is attacked or destroyed, one cannot die, for part of the soul remains earthbound and undamaged. But of course, existence in such a form… Death would be preferable. …Splitting [one's soul] is an act of violation…[done through] an act of evil…By committing murder. Killing rips the soul apart.

Voldemort is not content to create just one Horcrux; he creates six, with the seventh part of his soul remaining in his body. Horcruxes are what preserve him when he fails to kill the infant Harry. Such earthly immortality is what the Death Eaters mean by defeating death.

The Horcrux is the ultimate symbol of the crass materialist. Dumbledore tells Harry that, when Voldemort was still in school, he "was doing all he could to find out how to make himself immortal" on earth. This reveals a pathological fear of death. Significantly, a Horcrux places a piece of one's soul within an object. Dumbledore notes that Voldemort was not content to use just any object to hold pieces of his soul. He "preferred objects with a powerful magical history. ...Voldemort would have chosen his Horcruxes with some care, favoring objects worthy of the honor." This shows an obsession with objects. And the creation of each Horcrux requires a new murder, the ultimate form of treating people as objects.

Rowling sees the three elements of the Horcrux as naturally connected. If an obsession with objects is a sort of crass materialism, then an infatuation with earthly immortality is another form of it. An unhealthy obsession with physical objects matches an unhealthy obsession with one's physical body at the expense of the values of consciousness. If one sees people as material objects, then one will have few reservations about abusing them. Voldemort, who fears death above all else, is unable to love. Driven by fear of death and hatred of those who stand in his way, Voldemort abuses and murders others for his own depraved ends.

Supernaturalism and Death

How does one avoid a pathological fear of death? Chapter One suggests the most powerful answer welling up from Rowling's books: the heroic valuer realizes that only a life of virtue and loving friendship is worth living. While the heroic valuer does not walk through the shadow of death for ephemeral reasons, the hero does realize that, in order to protect one's highest values, sometimes one must give up lesser values or even risk one's life.

Yet Rowling offers another alternative to the pathological fear of death: a belief in the immortal soul. In Rowling's books, those capable of love and of risking their own lives for others share a common belief in life after death in a supernatural realm. This is a belief that Voldemort does not share. Thus, in Rowling's world, a belief in life after death is a natural partner of love. After all, if one thinks that the soul survives the body and finds a new supernatural home, one will not be quite as worried about losing one's body for the sake of a friend.

Several passages throughout the Potter books reveal Rowling's understanding of immortality.

Near the end of the first book, Dumbledore tells Harry that "to the well-organized mind, death is but the next great adventure."

In the fight at the end of *Order of the Phoenix*, one of Voldemort's Death Eaters kills Sirius Black. Harry seeks comfort from one of the ghosts who resides at Hogwarts. The ghost tells Harry that Sirius "will have…gone on." However, the ghost does not know about life after death so far as any non-earthly realm is concerned: "I was afraid of death…I chose to remain behind. …I know nothing of the secrets of death, Harry, for I chose my feeble imitation of life instead."

Hermione says in the seventh book, "Look, if I picked up a sword right now, Ron, and ran you through with it, I wouldn't damage your soul at all. …Whatever happens to your body, your soul will survive, untouched."

On Christmas Eve, Harry arrives at the tomb of his parents. The headstone reads, "The last enemy that shall be destroyed is death." Hermione explains, "It doesn't mean defeating death in the way the Death Eaters mean it, Harry…It means…living beyond death. Living after death."

Rowling has said of her books:

> To me, the religious parallels have always been obvious. But I never wanted to talk too openly about it because I thought it might show people who just wanted the story where we were going. …But I think those two particular quotations [Harry] finds on the tombstones [including the quote above]…they sum up, they almost epitomise, the whole series. …On any given moment if you asked me if I believe in life after death, I think if you polled me regularly through the week, I think I would come down on the side of yes—that I do believe in life after death. But it's something I wrestle with a lot. It preoccupies me a lot, and I think that's very obvious within the books.[29]

Rowling suggests that her heroes avoid an unhealthy fear of death by accepting life after death as a fact. But would it really matter in terms of the fundamental motivations of the characters if they did not believe in life after death? Again, Rowling presents virtuous heroes acting bravely in order to protect their own values. These values include friends, loved ones, and the ability to live and work in peace. These are the values relevant within the context of a normal human life.

A belief in the immortality of the soul is not necessary to live a healthy, loving life and to avoid a pathological fear of death. A heroic valuer needs no supernaturalist beliefs to motivate a virtuous life filled with love. While Rowling establishes that her heroes believe in the immortality of the soul, she doesn't establish that such a belief makes much difference in their motivations. The possibility of life after death is simply irrelevant.

A good person who pursues life-enhancing values normally will accept the fact of mortality. One who does not believe in life after death may be especially motivated to make the most of life on earth—to live the longest, richest, happiest life possible. While some people might live to be very old indeed, no one lives forever. There is no reason for either the fact of mortality or a disbelief in life after death to lead to immoral actions, domination of others, an obsession with objects, a pathological fear of death, or any of the other evils that plague Voldemort and his followers.

Neither does bravery fall apart absent a belief in life after death. Bravery enables one to protect and promote one's values here on earth. If anything, a belief in life after death serves as a deterrent to courageous action. After all, why defend one's life and values here on earth when life after death is (by various accounts) so much better? What accounts for bravery is a commitment to important values. The most that can be said in defense of a belief in life after death is that it does not necessarily lead to cowardice in life.

The events of Rowling's books actually demonstrate that "there are things worth dying for" even if one believes that physical death is the end. Indeed, Harry recognizes that some things are worse than death. After the centaur Firenze explains to Harry the evil of killing a unicorn, Harry asks, "But who'd be that desperate? ...If you're going to be cursed forever, death's better, isn't it?" Harry's insight does not depend on a belief in life after death; death is better than a cursed life on earth, even if death is the absolute end of a person. Dumbledore expresses a similar view. When Voldemort says, "There is nothing worse than death," Dumbledore replies, "You are quite wrong...Indeed, your failure to understand that there are things much worse than death has always been your greatest weakness." Voldemort, in creating the Horcruxes, becomes a mass murderer who destroys all of the values that make life worth living.

Linking Materialism, Independence, and Sacrifice

As second-handers tend to fall into crass materialism, so first-handers tend to avoid it. The first-hander relies on his or her own rational judgment and so at least implicitly recognizes the fundamental importance of one's rational consciousness. Thus the first-hander tends to adopt values appropriate to a rational, conscious being and acquire the knowledge needed to achieve those values. The first-hander relates physical objects to the values of consciousness and also treats other people as rational beings. It is no surprise that heroes such as Harry and Hermione think independently and develop strong friendships and healthy attitudes toward objects.

The second-hander, in contrast, neglects to make independent, rational judgments. The second-hander thus loses sight of the importance of consciousness. The second-hander fails to relate objects to his or her nature as a conscious being, and the second-hander also overlooks the fact that other people possess a rational consciousness. This leads to obsessing over objects and treating other people as objects. It is no surprise that villains such as Draco Malfoy base their values and opinions on social standards and at the same time mistreat others. The common problem is a failure to recognize the importance of rational consciousness. Because Draco does not rely on his own independent mind to evaluate facts and values, he is incapable of respecting other people as independent thinkers and valuers.

The discussion of death also ties to the discussion of Christian sacrifice from Chapter Four. Rowling seems to suggest a negative, symbolic link between the Horcrux and Christianity. While the central icon of Christianity is the cross, the symbol of Christ's love and sacrifice for mankind, "Horcrux" may be translated as a "filth cross" (see "hor" and "crux" in *The Oxford English Dictionary)*. I suspect that Rowling consciously made this connection; regardless, the association is an interesting one. If the cross for Rowling signifies love, self-sacrifice, spiritual values, and life after death, then the Horcrux signifies hatred, other-sacrifice, crass materialism, and a pathological fear of death.

However, I suggest that neither the cross nor the Horcrux is the appropriate symbol for the heroic valuer, who loves friends for their virtues and defends them from enemies, sacrifices neither self nor others, appreciates values both of consciousness and body, and lives life to the fullest even in the face of death. By my reading, this view of the heroic valuer is most consistent with the heroes of Rowling's magical world.

Even though various readers find inspiration in the Harry Potter books because of their themes of self-sacrifice and immortality, I have suggested that these elements are minor and mostly negated by the dominant theme of the heroic valuer. Readers are free to examine the evidence that I have presented and draw their own conclusions. Yet I think that there is one thing that all fans of Harry Potter can agree upon: Rowling herself is justly immortalized—through her work.

Conclusion
Mischief Managed

DUMBLEDORE WRITES IN HIS WILL, "To Miss Hermione Jean Granger, I leave my copy of *The Tales of Beedle the Bard*, in the hope that she will find it entertaining and instructive." Minister Scrimgeour wrongly assumes that the book contains coded messages from Dumbledore. Not long after Ron angrily abandons his friends, Harry finds the anguished Hermione "curled up in one of the sagging armchairs" with the book. Later, she asserts that the book's story of the Hallows is "about how humans are frightened of death." She is partly right. It is a morality tale, but in her world it also describes magical objects of great power that actually exist.

Rowling's novels certainly entertain and instruct, and they too deal partly with the human fear of death. The obvious difference is that the novels do not describe real magical objects through symbolic stories. Rowling invokes Christian supernaturalism and alludes to the Biblical clash between Satan and the Son of God, and in that sense Rowling writes in allegories. Yet these religious stories are well-known to the reader; Rowling promises no unique or hidden mystical understanding.

One reason Rowling's books prove so exciting is that they continually reveal new levels of connections. For example, Harry's

Invisibility Cloak from the first book turns out to be one of the Hallows of the final book. As interesting as this is literarily, it also introduces a subtle risk for the reader. The novels do not offer the reader mysterious magical insight the way that Dumbledore's *Tales* do for Hermione. The temptation, then, is to become wrapped up in the details of the Potter stories and neglect the more abstract ways that they translate to Muggle life, to get caught up in the imaginary magic and overlook the real thing.

Novels are not merely morality tales. The point of literature is not primarily to teach, but to bring alive the writer's ideals in concrete form through lifelike characters acting over a series of connected events. In doing this, literature can incidentally teach valuable lessons, but these lessons are not as obvious as finding the hidden powers of secret objects. Such abstract lessons must be thoughtfully applied to the concretes of daily life.

Ayn Rand aptly describes Rowling's type of literature in her 1968 introduction to *The Fountainhead*:

> It deals, not with the random trivia of the day, but with the timeless, fundamental, universal problems and *values* of human existence. It does not record or photograph; it creates and projects. It is concerned—in the words of Aristotle—not with things as they are, but with things as they might be and ought to be.[30]

Any novel that deals in values and things as they ought to be potentially offers important lessons for living our lives. As I've indicated, Rowling gets a great deal right in her treatment of values and offers profoundly important lessons.

As Muggles, we are not destined to fly by broom, duel with wands, or ride dragons. Yet the deeper magic of Harry Potter flows through our world, too. It is the magic of sharing friendships, finding love, and building families. Enjoying a fine sporting match, laughing at a well-crafted joke, and savoring an elegant dance. Finding inspiration in a great hero or mentor with the stature of Dumbledore and recognizing the goodness in a tragically misunderstood figure such as Snape. Developing our unique talents and skills and preparing for our futures with hope and anticipation.

Such magic must not be shelved when the books are closed. Readers of Rowling's fiction appropriately allow the stories to inspire them to seriously consider their values, discover the courage to fight for those values, think and live according to the judgment of their independent minds, and accept moral responsibility for their choices. There is no O.W.L., no Voldemort, no Vernon Dursley, no Hallow, but there are important studies and milestones, serious threats to our values, temptations to fall into dependence and petty obsessions, and sources of power that can be respected or abused. Even when Rowling's themes clash, as I've suggested they do with heroism versus sacrifice and immortality, they inspire the reader to independently evaluate these issues in greater depth, for they profoundly inform our values.

Millions of readers have responded with such tremendous enthusiasm to the Harry Potter books in large measure because they vividly show the heroic valuer in action. Rowling has done what few modern authors dare—she has challenged her readers to moral excellence. The world could use more heroes. A hero is what J. K. Rowling's brilliant vision beckons the reader to become.

Part Three
Additional Essays

THE ORIGINAL EDITION OF THIS BOOK was published in 2008. That text, including the pagination through page 98, remains here exactly as it was in the original. I remain pleased with that work and find no reason to alter it.

In this expanded edition, I take up a number of themes that I neglected in 2008. I am quite glad that I waited to write about the psychological elements of the novels, for J. K. Rowling's more recent comments about her own life shed light on the psychology of her stories.

As a political writer, I noticed the political backdrop of the stories, so I am pleased to address wizarding government in more detail here. See the second new essay, "Wizard Law and Segregation."

The other essays have been published before, though I've substantially rewritten several of them for this expanded edition. These essays discuss the news media, *The Tales of Beedle the Bard*, J. R. R. Tolkien and Lloyd Alexander (two of my childhood favorites), "Harry Potter's Lessons for Muggle Politicians," the parallels between Rowling and Ayn Rand, and the Potter films. I hope other Harry Potter fans enjoy reading the essays; I deeply enjoyed writing them.[31]

Essay One

The Psychology of Harry Potter

J. K. Rowling "had leanings towards depression from quite an early age."[32] She also experienced "suicidal thoughts" following her separation from her first husband, between the years when she first conceived the Harry Potter story and when she saw her first novel published.[33] Moreover, soon after Rowling imagined her fantasy world, her mother died of a degenerative disease.[34] It comes as little surprise, then, that Rowling's novels offer psychologically complex material. Before exploring the novels, we turn briefly to Rowling's public comments about difficult periods of her own past, for then the connection between her life and her art becomes evident.

Rowling describes her depression: "It is that absence of feeling, that absence of hope. You don't know you can feel better. It is so difficult to describe to someone who hasn't been there, because it isn't sadness. Sadness is not a bad thing, to cry, to feel."[35] Rowling adds, "Mid-twenties life circumstances were poor and I really plummeted…The thing that made me go for help…was probably my daughter. She was something that earthed me, grounded me, and I thought, this isn't right…she cannot grow up with me in this state."[36]

Rowling says her depression was "characterized for me by a numbness, a coldness, an inability to believe that you will feel happy again, or that you could feel lighthearted again. It's just all the color drained out of life, really." She adds that she became fearful about her daughter: "I loved Jessica very very much and was terrified something was going to happen to her. ...I'd gone into that very depressive mindset where everything has gone wrong so this one good thing in my life will now go wrong as well. So it was almost a surprise to me every morning that she was still alive. I kept expecting her to die. It was a bad bad time." Rowling notes that her sense of loss stemming from the death of her mother "seeped into every part of the books."[37]

Rowling, then, saw her mother die and feared the death of her daughter, experienced a cold and unhappy depression, and for her daughter found the strength to seek help.

It would be a mistake to look at the psychology of the novels only in relation to Rowling's life. The psychological material contributes to the broader themes of the novels, and it provides worthwhile lessons in its own right. Those insights would be well worth exploring even if we knew nothing about Rowling's past. Thus, the primary goal here is to understand the nature and significance of the psychology of the Potter series as it functions in Rowling's literature. However, given that Rowling chose to discuss her personal history with depression, noting the similarities between Rowling's experiences and her art helps to illuminate both.

Dementors and Patronuses

Others have noticed the parallels between Rowling's life and her novels; for example, Adeel Amini, writing for a student newspaper in Edinburgh, notes that depression finds "a strong metaphor…in the Harry Potter series through the Dementors."[38] The dementors guard Azkaban prison for the Ministry of Magic, and they readily serve the evil Lord Voldemort when he rises to power.

Harry first meets a dementor on the train to school in *Prisoner of Azkaban*:

> Its face was completely hidden beneath its hood. ...There was a hand protruding from the cloak and it was glistening,

grayish, slimy-looking, and scabbed, like something dead that had decayed in water. ...And then the thing beneath the hood, whatever it was, drew a long, slow, rattling breath, as though it were trying to suck something more than air from its surroundings. An intense cold swept over them all. Harry felt his own breath catch in his chest. The cold went deeper than his skin. It was inside his chest, it was inside his very heart. ...He was drowning in cold. ...He was being dragged downward, the roaring growing louder.

While Harry's friends do not succumb to the torturous force of the dementors as completely as Harry does, Neville feels their coldness, and Ron says, "I felt weird. ...Like I'd never be cheerful again."

While playing a Quidditch match Harry meets a pack of dementors who show up unexpectedly: "It was as though freezing water were rising in his chest, cutting at his insides. And then he heard it again. ...Someone was screaming, screaming inside his head."

The dementors elicit in Harry the hidden memory of his mother's murder when he was an infant. Harry's professor Remus Lupin points out, "The dementors affect you worse than the others because there are horrors in your past that the others don't have"—the horrors of seeing his parents murdered.

Lupin further explains:

> Dementors...infest the darkest, filthiest places, they glory in decay and despair, they drain peace, hope and happiness out of the air around them. ...Get too near a dementor and every good feeling, every happy memory will be sucked out of you. If it can, the dementor will feed on you long enough to reduce you to something like itself...soulless and evil. You'll be left with nothing but the worst experiences of your life.

When a dementor completely overpowers its victim, it delivers the "Dementor's Kiss"; dementors "clamp their jaws upon the mouth of the victim and...suck out his soul," Lupin explains.

"You'll have no sense of self anymore, no memory, no…anything. There's no chance at all of recovery. You'll just—exist. As an empty shell. And your soul is gone forever…lost."

Harry seeks Lupin's help with fighting off the dementors largely to avoid another debilitating incident on the Quidditch field. Thus, Harry focuses on a concrete goal, something important to him, to find the motivation to overcome the dementors.

How does one fight dementors? Comfort food can help somewhat; after Harry first encounters a dementor Lupin gives him a "large piece" from "an enormous slab of chocolate," saying, "Eat it. It'll help." Chocolate is an example of a simple, sensual pleasure that can help bring one's mind back to pleasant thoughts and the task of living.

To truly beat back the dementors, however, a wizard must conjure a Patronus Charm. A Patronus "is a kind of anti-dementor—a guardian that acts as a shield between you and the dementor," Lupin explains. The professor continues: "The Patronus is a kind of positive force, a projection of the very things that the dementor feeds upon—hope, happiness, the desire to survive." One can conjure a Patronus "only if you are concentrating, with all your might, on a single, very happy memory."

Harry settles on the "very happy memory" of first riding a broomstick. This produces a "silvery gas" but fails to defeat the image of a dementor. Harry again fails when he thinks of winning a school championship; he instead becomes overwhelmed by memories of his father fighting Voldemort before perishing. On his third try, Harry remembers finding out he is a wizard, and this produces a "silver shadow" that stands "between him and the dementor."

Near the end of the book, when much more than a Quidditch match is on the line—the dementors swarm in to suck the souls out of Harry and his godfather—Harry finally discovers the full power of a Patronus. Initially he believes his father will somehow return to stop the dementors. Finally Harry realizes that it is he, not his father, who must produce the Patronus. He conjures his most powerful Patronus, "not a shapeless cloud of mist, but a blinding, dazzling, silver animal," a stag, the image of his father. Later Professor Dumbledore explains, "You think the dead we loved ever truly leave us? You think that we don't recall them more clearly than ever in times of great trouble? Your father is alive in you, Harry, and shows himself most plainly when you have need of him."

Dementors and Patronuses obviously relate to depression and Rowling's experiences with it. Like the dementors, depression can make one feel cold and lifeless, like one's soul is being sucked out. Thinking of happy things and enjoying the little pleasures of life (like chocolate) can help restore a positive outlook. Focusing on one's goals, whether winning a sports match, writing a novel, or raising a daughter, can feed the incentive to overcome the depressing dementors. By seeking help, whether from a trusted professor or from cognitive behavioral therapy, which Rowling pursued, one can find the inner strength to beat back the demons. Finally, the most powerful Patronus comes from thoughts of loved ones, such as one's father or daughter.

In the case of the Patronus Charm, the magic of Rowling's novels perfectly mirrors the psychological help we may give ourselves and seek from others. Fighting the dementors requires specific psychological strategies and, more importantly, the will to implement them.

Boggarts

While depression can become a soul-sucking threat to one's very life, other psychological hazards pose less of a challenge, such as imaginary monsters under the bed. Still we must learn to deal with such fears. That is the main lesson Professor Lupin teaches with a boggart, "a shape-shifter" that "can take the shape of whatever it thinks will frighten us most," as Hermione explains.

Lupin points out, "It's always best to have company when you're dealing with a boggart. He becomes confused. Which should he become, a headless corpse or a flesh-eating slug?" Any child who asks to sleep in his parents' room knows company can keep such fears at bay. As adults, we share our fears with others so that we can reflect on them and gain the insight of friends. Whether we are afraid of something at work, an aspect of parenting, or a health issue, talking over our fears with others can help keep them in context and keep us focused on solutions rather than our fears.

Company helps, but "the thing that really finishes a boggart is *laughter*. What you need to do is force it to assume a shape that you find amusing," Lupin explains. Fittingly, the charm for defeating a boggart is pronouncing "riddikulus." However, "the word alone is not enough," Lupin emphasizes; one must imagine the object of one's fears in a ridiculous state. For example, Neville (Harry's classmate) imagines Professor Snape, whom he fears, wearing a silly combination of his grandmother's clothes.

Primarily a boggart represents a fear mostly created by the mind, rather than a fear based in real danger. Neville fears a stern teacher; other students fear a mummy, a banshee, a creeping severed hand, and a giant spider. For these sorts of fears, company and laughter work the magic.

Sometimes, however, a boggart can reflect something that does pose a genuine danger. Lupin, for instance, sees in the boggart an image of the moon; as a werewolf during the full moon Lupin loses his faculties and becomes dangerous unless he takes the right potion. After Voldemort's rise, Harry finds Molly Weasley with a boggart that has taken the form of her worst fears: her own children, dead.

Lupin is surprised that Harry sees a dementor rather than Voldemort in the boggart. Lupin says, "I'm impressed. ...That suggests that what you fear most of all is—fear. Very wise, Harry." What are we to make of this?

Rowling's use of the boggart, the dementor, and Voldemort suggests several levels of fear. A boggart can present itself as something that we fear but that does not actually pose any real danger, such as an imaginary monster under the bed. Such fears recede in cheerful company and contemplation of how the fears have no real basis (they are ridiculous). A dementor, on the other hand, represents depression, an internal, psychologically based danger that can, if unchecked, destroy one's life. Voldemort represents an external evil that can (as Molly realizes) cause mayhem and death; it is perfectly reasonable to fear Voldemort.

Harry does not become overwhelmed by dementors, for he can produce a Patronus to fight them. However, he remains afraid of them, a fear manifest in the boggart. Harry fears the debilitating dementors even more than he fears Voldemort, for dementors incapacitate their victims and make action against external dangers impossible. Lupin's comment to Harry suggests that dementors feed on uncontrolled fears and promote a universalized fear of losing life's most important values—in Rowling's case, a daughter.

The Mirror and the Stone

Though not as destructive as severe depression, prolonged melancholy over lost loved ones can disrupt one's life. While Rowling certainly says nothing against mourning the dead, something a loving person must do, she does warn against obsessing over them. Rowling represents this idea through the Mirror of Erised and the Resurrection Stone.

The Mirror of Erised, which Harry discovers while wandering around Hogwarts castle his first year, shows one's "heart's desire." Harry sees his parents. He finds the mirror increasingly alluring; on his third night observing it, he becomes tempted to stay. "There was nothing to stop him from staying here all night with his family. Nothing at all."

Fortunately, Dumbledore interrupts Harry. Dumbledore explains that "the happiest man on earth" would "see himself exactly as he is" in the mirror. For others, the mirror shows the "most desperate desire of our hearts. You, who have never known your family, see them standing around you." Dumbledore warns: "However, this mirror will give us neither knowledge or truth. Men have wasted away before it, entranced by what they have seen, or been driven mad, not knowing if what it shows is real or even possible." Dumbledore reminds Harry, "It does not do to dwell on dreams and forget to live, remember that."

In contrast with the mirror is an album of wizard photographs, mostly of his mother and father, that Harry receives as a present. This shows the difference between a dangerous preoccupation with death and a healthy remembrance of loved ones.

A magical object with similar properties appears in *Deathly Hallows*. We learn of the Resurrection Stone through "The Tale of the Three Brothers," a children's story recited by Hermione. The premise is that, after three magical brothers cheat Death by building a bridge over a raging river, Death offers each a wish, hoping to trick them into picking something foolish.

> Then the second brother, who was an arrogant man, decided that he wanted to humiliate Death still further, and asked for the power to recall others from Death. So Death picked up a stone from the riverbank and gave it to the second brother, and told him that the stone would have the power to bring back the dead.

Predictably, this gift works out badly for the brother:

> The second brother journeyed to his own home, where he lived alone. Here he took out the stone that had the power to recall the dead, and turned it thrice in his hand. To his amazement and his delight, the figure of the girl he had once hoped to marry, before her untimely death, appeared at once before him.

> Yet she was sad and cold, separated from him as by a veil. Though she had returned to the mortal world, she did not truly belong there and suffered. Finally the second brother, driven mad with hopeless longing, killed himself so as truly to join her.

Again these symbols hold obvious relevance for real life. People do not need magical mirrors or stones to dwell obsessively on what they have lost. Of course losing a loved one can devastate a person for a time and leave lasting emotional scars. But we cannot bring back the dead, whether through magical objects or intense longing. We must find a way to go on living and appreciate the loved ones who remain with us.

The Scar of Evil

Through the dementors, the boggarts, and the magical mirror and stone, Rowling tracks the psychology of depression, fear, and preoccupation with the dead. Another powerful psychological theme running throughout the Potter series is the temptation or allure of evil and the fear of falling into that temptation. The most poignant symbol of that allure is Harry's scar, which he acquires when Voldemort tries but fails to murder him.

Soon after Voldemort murders Harry's parents, Dumbledore sees on Harry's forehead "a curiously shaped cut, like a bolt of lighting," caused by the violence. Harry learns that his scar is more than just a patch of blemished skin. When early in the first novel Professors Quirrell and Snape discuss Harry, "a sharp, hot pain shot across the scar on Harry's forehead." Later, when Harry sees a cloaked figure drinking unicorn blood—a great evil—"a pain like he'd never felt before pierced his head; it was as though his scar were on fire." Harry's scar continues to cause him pain, and he believes "it's a warning" that "means danger's coming."

Finally Harry discovers that Quirrell seeks to restore Voldemort to power. Quirrell's touch again causes Harry's scar to hurt, as though his head "was about to split in two." But something unexpected happens when Quirrell grabs Harry: the touch causes Quirrell agonizing pain as his skin burns. Later Dumbledore explains why: Harry's mother died trying to save him, and such a love "leaves its own mark." This mark is "not a scar"; it leaves "no visible sign." But "to have been loved so deeply, even though the person who loved us is gone, will give us some protection forever."

Harry is thus doubly marked as an infant. Voldemort's attack leaves a visible scar on his forehead, something that pains him in the presence of evil, yet Harry's mother leaves her own invisible mark of love that helps protect Harry from evil.

During his second year at school, Harry discovers another connection with evil, besides his scar—he can hear a voice threatening to kill people. The threatening voice leads Harry to the scene of a crime: the petrification of the caretaker's cat.

Harry learns that the voice comes from a giant snake, and he worries about his ability to understand it. Harry shares the ability to speak snake language with Salazar Slytherin, the ancient founder of the Hogwarts house to which Voldemort belongs. Finally, when Harry meets an image of a young Voldemort, who as a youth went by the name Tom Riddle, Voldemort comments: "There are strange likenesses between us...Both half-bloods [with only one magical parent], orphans, raised by Muggles [non-magical people]." Voldemort notes they both speak snake language, and, he adds, "We even *look* something alike."

Harry grows disturbed by his superficial similarities to Voldemort. Dumbledore explains to Harry, "[Voldemort] transferred some of his own powers to you the night he gave you that scar." Harry rightly reiterates that Voldemort "put a bit of himself" into Harry. However, Dumbledore continues, the similarities between Voldemort and Harry are not what really matter: "It is our choices, Harry, that show what we truly are, far more than our abilities." Even though he was indeed marked by evil, through the scar and the powers Harry shares with Voldemort, the scar does not dictate his course.

Following Voldemort's return to power—an event that brutalized Harry and allowed Voldemort to murder one of Harry's friends—Harry struggles with anger and dreams of Voldemort. Both his anger and his dreams seem to further tie Harry to evil.

Harry grows so angry with his seemingly inattentive friends that he throws away their gifts unopened; his anger evokes memories of seeing Voldemort rise to power and murder his friend. Harry suffers recurring nightmares as a result of that horrific encounter with Voldemort.

His problems compounding, Harry finds himself "consumed with anger and frustration, grinding his teeth and clenching his fists." When Harry is reunited with his friends, he yells at them. When he considers how Dumbledore cut him off from information, his "insides burn with anger again." As school begins Harry lashes out at his friends, and he also lets his temper run away with him in class.

Harry's connection to Voldemort deepens through his dreams and his scar. Harry dreams of Voldemort's desires, and the dreams "made his scar prickle." When Harry is awake, his scar hurts when Voldemort is especially angry or when he is pleased. As Harry drifts into yet another fitful sleep haunted by Voldemort, he wonders, "*Why* did he know what Voldemort was feeling? What was this weird connection between them?"

Finally Harry dreams that he is a snake attacking Arthur Weasley, the father of his friend Ron. But this is no mere dream; Voldemort's snake had attacked Arthur, and Harry had seen it in his dream, causing his scar to again throb in pain. This time Harry's feeling of living through the snake lingers in waking life; as he talks with Dumbledore, Harry experiences an intense hatred, "unbidden, unwanted, but terrifyingly strong," urging him to "sink his fangs into the man before him."

After Dumbledore sends Harry to Professor Snape for special training, Snape explains:

> The curse that failed to kill you seems to have forged some kind of connection between you and the Dark Lord. The evidence suggests that at times, when your mind is most relaxed and vulnerable—when you are asleep, for instance—you are sharing the Dark Lord's thoughts and emotions.

Snape confirms Harry's fear that, through this mysterious connection, Voldemort might compel Harry to act viciously.

Snape offers Harry some advice in preventing Voldemort from reading his thoughts and controlling his mind: resist, remain focused and controlled, "let go of all emotion," don't "wallow in sad memories," "control your anger, discipline your mind."

But Harry does not succeed in blocking Voldemort from his mind, and eventually, through a dream, Voldemort tricks him and his friends into walking into a trap. During the resulting confrontation Voldemort briefly possesses Harry.

After the fight that results in the death of Harry's beloved godfather Sirius Black, Dumbledore explains the significance of Harry's emotions. Though Harry continues to struggle with "white-hot anger," it is his love for Sirius and others that saves him. "The fact that you can feel pain like this" over Sirius's death, Dumbledore explains, "is your greatest strength."

In a rage, Harry declares that he does not want human feelings any more, but Dumbledore is not fooled. "You do care," he tells Harry; "You care so much you feel as though you will bleed to death with the pain of it." Dumbledore again reminds Harry that his scar is "the sign of a connection forged between [Harry] and Voldemort." However, the other mark—the mark of love—saves Harry from Voldemort.

Dumbledore continues:

> That power [of love] took you to save Sirius tonight. That power also saved you from possession by Voldemort, because he could not bear to reside in a body so full of the force he detests. In the end, it mattered not that you could not close your mind. It was your heart that saved you.

In the final book of the series, Harry continues to struggle with the pain of his scar and visions of Voldemort's actions. However, when his friend Dobby gives his life to save Harry and his friends, Harry learns to master the scar:

> His scar burned, but he was master of the pain; he felt it, yet was apart from it. He had learned control at last, learned to shut his mind to Voldemort... Just as Voldemort had not been able to possess Harry while Harry was consumed with grief for Sirius, so his thoughts could not

penetrate Harry now, while he mourned Dobby. Grief, it seemed, drove Voldemort out…though Dumbledore, of course, would have said that it was love.

Finally, through Snape's memory of Dumbledore, Harry learns the deeper significance of the scar:

> On the night Lord Voldemort tried to kill him, when Lily cast her own life between them as a shield, the Killing Curse rebounded upon Lord Voldemort, and a fragment of Voldemort's soul was blasted apart from the whole, and latched itself onto the only living soul left in that collapsing building. Part of Lord Voldemort lives inside Harry, and it is that which gives him the power of speech with snakes, and a connection with Lord Voldemort's mind…And while that fragment of soul, unmissed by Voldemort, remains attached to and protected by Harry, Lord Voldemort cannot die.

While only Harry carries a piece of Voldemort's soul, others experience a comparable temptation of evil. Ron Weasley suffers the torments of a Horcrux, a magical object containing another piece of Voldemort's soul, as does Ron's sister Ginny. The Horcrux appears to Ron as Hermione, whom Ron loves, only the Horcrux version taunts Ron, preying on his deepest fears, and says she prefers Harry.

Harry begins to drive out Voldemort through his love for Sirius and Dobby, and he finishes the job by risking his life out of love for all his friends. When Harry confronts Voldemort, the evil wizard curses him, knocking him unconscious. Harry enters a dreamlike state in which he is able to commune with Dumbledore, who explains that Harry remains alive. Harry answers, "But I should have died—I didn't defend myself! I meant to let him kill me!" Dumbledore replies, "And that will, I think, have made all the difference."

Instead of killing Harry, as Voldemort intends, the dark wizard instead destroys the piece of his own soul that had latched onto Harry. What makes this possible was that, in restoring his powers, Voldemort took Harry's blood, thereby taking in Lily's protective power for her son. Voldemort "took into his body a tiny part of the enchantment your mother laid upon you when she died for you," Dumbledore explains.

The story makes for remarkable and powerful literature and no less remarkable psychology. What is the relationship between the fiction and real-life psychology in this case?

In the novels, Voldemort is a real and powerful evil wizard, whom Harry must defeat. I propose that, as a psychological symbol, the scar Voldemort gives to Harry represents a person's desire to do evil. This desire is not inborn; it can arise from a deep-seated anger about some injustice or horrible event, an anger that can grow into a generalized malevolence toward the world.

Harry takes on the perspective of Voldemort in his dreams and visions; this is much like someone imagining possible evil acts. What saves a person from enacting such evil is love—love for one's life and values, notably other people. By betraying love for others and letting anger explode out of control, one can deepen one's bond with evil and ultimately become possessed by it. Harry contains his anger and prevents Voldemort from taking him over by remembering his love for his deceased friends and mother and maintaining loving relationships with others.

Harry carries two marks with him from birth: the mark of his mother's love and the mark of Voldemort's evil. Each of us has the same capacity to choose love and values or to choose hatred and the destruction of values.

In fiction, Voldemort is a demonic figure of immense power bent on destroying virtuous people and controlling what's left of the world. As a psychological symbol, Voldemort is the potential allure of blind rage, violence, mayhem, and ultimately murder. As Rowling clung to love for her daughter, so we can embrace our own loving relationships to escape those scars threatening to draw us into evil.

A Return to Values

I have argued that the dominant theme of the Potter novels is the heroic fight for life-serving values. The psychological lessons of the novels show that dementors, boggarts, magical mirrors and stones, and scars of evil—that is, depression, debilitating fears, a preoccupation with death, and the temptation to fall into hatred and destruction—can interfere with our pursuit of those values.

Through allegory, Rowling illustrates some of our major barriers to psychological health and some powerful techniques for overcoming those barriers. We can begin to defeat depression by contemplating all the positive things that enrich our lives, relishing the pleasures life has to offer, focusing on our goals and values, seeking experienced help when needed, and remembering our loved ones. (This is not to understate the profound and often prolonged difficulties in dealing with clinical depression.) We can defeat our unfounded or exaggerated fears by sharing good company and recognizing when our fears break loose from reality. We can remember lost loved ones in a healthy way and continue to live for values. And we can recognize our potential to respond to frustration and tragedy with blinding anger and destruction. We can instead focus on our loved ones and a life of values.

In publicly discussing her difficult past, Rowling sheds light on the psychological themes of her novels. Through her work she shares some powerful psychological insights for pursuing our own lives and happiness more successfully.

Essay Two
Wizard Law and Segregation

To achieve her fantasy scenario in which the wizard world coexists with the regular human (Muggle) world, J. K. Rowling must explain why and how these two worlds remain mostly separated. The primary mechanism is the "International Statute of Wizarding Secrecy," passed in 1689 "when wizardkind voluntarily went underground."[39] The law serves as a convenient plot device that allows Rowling to layer the wizard world atop our real world; thus, it would be a mistake to overemphasize the thematic importance of this law. However, under the law wizards enforce segregation from Muggles, so it is worth looking into, particularly as it seems to clash with Rowling's broader themes of political liberty.

Wizard Government

A brief review of wizard law and government will help set the context for wizard segregation.

Rowling's major political themes largely involve what happens when government becomes corrupt. Under Minister of Magic Cornelius Fudge, the Ministry censors the press, tries to railroad Harry on bogus charges, and meddles at Hogwarts school. Under Fudge's successor the Ministry arrests an innocent man for political purposes. Finally the Ministry falls to Voldemort's forces and becomes the instrument of murder and tyranny. (See Chapter Two of this book for more details.)

Even under normal circumstances, before the rise of Voldemort, the Ministry acts badly regarding other races. The government sanctions and enforces the major injustice of elf slavery, something Harry's friend Hermione fights. Likewise, the wizard government oppresses the giants, as it once brutalized the goblins, and it passes anti-werewolf legislation that harms Harry's friend and mentor Remus Lupin. Through her heroes Rowling clearly condemns all such cases of oppression.

Thankfully, the Ministry also serves the essential governmental function of protecting people (or at least wizards) from violence. Notably, the Ministry enforces laws against using the "Unforgivable Curses" of murder, torture, and control, the violation of which brings a life sentence in Azkaban prison. The Ministry's Aurors serve as a police force to catch dark wizards who disobey fundamental wizard law.

The Ministry serves a variety of other functions as well. While semiautonomous governors control Hogwarts school, the Ministry also helps run it (though it issues no compulsory attendance rule except under Voldemort's influence). The Ministry's Wizengamot tries wizards over infractions of various laws, sometimes including those restricting the use of magic by minors. The Ministry also maintains a Department of Mysteries, oversees major wizard sporting matches, commits disturbed wizards to St. Mungo's hospital, requires licenses for traveling by Apparation (which can be dangerous), and enforces laws against altering the past.

While Rowling's heroes readily respect the laws against harming others, they also routinely violate more mundane regulations. For example, while Hermione appreciates the importance of the laws governing time, she also willfully breaks the law in order to stop the Ministry from carrying out faulty sentences, and Dumbledore encourages her. During their student years, Harry's father and godfather illegally become unregistered Animagi, capable of turning into sentient animals. Though the Ministry outlaws the uncontrolled breeding of dragons, Hagrid hatches a baby dragon, which Harry and his friends help smuggle to safety. Fred and George Weasley purchase "Venomous Tentacula seeds" for use in their joke shop even though "they're a Class C Non-Tradeable Substance," and Harry knows about this and keeps it a secret. Despite some restrictions on underage drinking, Professor Slughorn offers Harry and Ron Weasley glasses of "oak-matured mead" in his school office.

Sometimes the heroes openly mock the government's work. For example, when Percy Weasley discusses his Ministry project on "trying to standardize cauldron thickness," Ron makes fun of his efforts.

Rowling, then, projects three basic attitudes toward government functions. The heroes respect the laws against harming others, they oppose obviously oppressive laws, and they remain ambivalent about laws regulating various behaviors, sometimes obeying such laws and sometimes flouting them. So, within the general framework of wizard law, what is the nature of wizard segregation?

Wizard Segregation

The impetus for wizard segregation, Dumbledore explains, was "the persecution of witches and wizards…gathering pace all over Europe in the early fifteenth century." Though "genuine witches and wizards were reasonably adept at escaping the stake, block, and noose…a number of deaths did occur."[40]

Another reason for segregation is to cut off the temptation of Muggles to rely on wizards' magic. Hagrid tells Harry that the Ministry's "main job is to keep it from the Muggles that there's still witches and wizards" around, because otherwise "everyone'd be wantin' magic solutions to their problems." Likewise, Dumbledore explains that the general attitude behind the secrecy statute was, "Let the Muggles manage without us!"[41]

The fact that Muggles sometimes bear magical children makes impossible the complete separation of the Muggle and magical worlds. The Muggles allowed to know about the wizard world include Harry's aunt and uncle, Harry's grandparents, and Hermione's parents. Moreover, the Ministry communicates with the British Prime Minister about Voldemort's threat.

The wizards keep nearly all Muggles in the dark about the existence of wizards and magic, however. The Ministry accomplishes this by altering the memories of Muggles exposed to magic, outlawing the enchantment of Muggle objects, and forbidding the practice of magic in front of Muggles. For example, the Ministry alters the memory of Muggles tortured by Voldemort's followers, and it accuses Harry of performing magic "in the presence of a Muggle." The Ministry also bans the importation of flying carpets, because "carpets are defined as a Muggle Artifact by the Registry of Proscribed Charmable Objects."

Ron explains that his father Arthur works for the Misuse of Muggle Artifacts Office:

> It's all to do with bewitching things that are Muggle-made, you know, in case they end up back in a Muggle shop or house. Like, last year, some old witch died and her tea set was sold to an antiques shop. This Muggle woman bought it, took it home…The teapot went berserk and squirted boiling tea all over the place and one man ended up in the hospital with the sugar tongs clamped to his nose. Dad was going frantic…and they had to do Memory Charms and all sorts of stuff to cover it up.

One evening Arthur's department conducts nine raids to find and confiscate illegally charmed Muggle objects; it finds "a few shrinking door keys and a biting kettle." Devious wizards charmed the keys for "Muggle-baiting," as each key "keeps shrinking to nothing so [Muggles] can never find it when" needed. However, the main purpose of the Ministry is to keep magic secret from Muggles, not protect Muggles from dangerous or irksome magic.

Like other heroes in the Potter series, Arthur treats the law with a wink, though his job is enforcing the law. For example, he charms a Muggle car so that it can fly. Arthur explains to his irritated wife that the law—which he helped write—offers a loophole; he can enchant the car so long as he does not intend to fly it. However, he reacts with glee when his sons fly the car to retrieve Harry, and he neglects to report the incident to the Ministry.

Oddly, while the Ministry enforces laws against using the Imperius charm to control others, the Ministry itself controls wizards and Muggles alike through other magical means to maintain segregation. Forcibly wiping someone's memories, without that person's consent, constitutes an extremely invasive form of control. While the Ministry sensibly prevents wizards from harming Muggles with enchanted objects, the Ministry also prevents wizards and Muggles from freely trading for mutual benefit.

Even though Rowling's heroes rail against bigotry against Muggles (and bigotry in general), the motivation for segregation seems to be rooted in soft bigotry against Muggles. Segregation presumes that Muggles in general would act badly toward wizards and become unhealthily dependent on magic. Yet Muggles have employed very similar sorts of arguments to rationalize segregation of Muggle communities.

Again, wizard segregation is a plot device, not a major theme of the novels. Literarily, the primary purpose of segregation is to make the fantasy fit with the real-world background. However, wizard segregation does seem to clash with Rowling's broader themes against bigotry and controlling people with magic.

Ultimately, wizard segregation points to the difficulties of merging worlds operating by fundamentally different physical laws; the integration of wizards and Muggles remains difficult to imagine. It is neither surprising nor particularly troubling that Rowling's solution to the problem—wizard segregation—generates a few residual problems.

Essay Three
News Media in Harry Potter

IN J. K. ROWLING'S HARRY POTTER SERIES of novels, the unethical journalist Rita Skeeter intentionally misrepresents quotes, employs deception to gather information, and smears subjects by dropping important context about them.

Unfortunately, one of Skeeter's signature techniques, dropping context, is on display in a real-life article about the Potter series published in 2008 by the *American Communication Journal*.[42] This is particularly ironic given that the article, written by lead author Amanda Sturgill in collaboration with Jessica Winney and Tina Libhart, condemns Skeeter as "the epitome of the corrupt, yellow journalist stereotype."

Moreover, by unfairly criticizing the Potter series in a media release, Sturgill promoted Skeeter-like headlines throughout the popular media. For example, one headline blared, "'Potter' Bad for Newspapers?"[43]

Sturgill and her coauthors claim of the novels, "The extremely negative depiction of journalism could have an adverse effect on child readers of the series as they may not have an understanding of journalism in a broader context." However, Sturgill's article actually demonstrates through its own errors, methodological flaws, and missing context that the critical skepticism toward media encouraged by the Potter series is entirely warranted. Furthermore, elements of the novels ignored by Sturgill's paper reveal a constructive view of journalism within the series.

Sturgill's False Ideal

Sturgill's article inappropriately contrasts the corrupt instances of journalism in the Potter series with a nonexistent perfect ideal. The paper's abstract states that, "given the prevalence of tabloid journalism and 'entertainment' news," children may fail to understand "true journalistic integrity." The paper continues, "The ideal goal of journalism is to ensure an informed citizenry in an objective and truthful manner."

However, in the real world, journalism often falls short of its "true integrity" and ideals, and the Potter series properly encourages readers to become aware of this fact.

As Sturgill's paper grants, children are in fact inundated with "tabloid journalism and 'entertainment' news"; they often see it whenever the television is on or whenever they walk through a grocery line.

Sturgill's paper complains that, in the Potter series, "individuals within the government" leak "information to the press" and seek publicity "to influence how subjects are perceived in print"—practices that are prevalent in real-life journalism.

Even higher orders of journalism often fail. A few illustrative examples should suffice to secure the point.

- In 2001, the *Denver Post* reported that the local Anti-Defamation League was "looking into" the political activism of Bob Glass (a friend of mine).[44] The paper neglected to mention that Glass is Jewish and that some of his relatives died in the Holocaust.
- In 2003, Jayson Blair, while working for the *New York Times*, among the most prestigious newspapers in the world, "committed frequent acts of journalistic fraud while covering significant news events," as the paper itself later admitted.[45]

- In 2008, the *Denver Post* published an article with claims about studies of children's health insurance. Unfortunately, when I asked about the studies, they did not in fact support the author's statements, as Dave Kopel pointed out in an article for a competing newspaper.[46] (I selected two examples from the *Denver Post* simply because it is the paper I most closely follow.)

- In 2011, following a mass murder and attempted assassination of Representative Gabrielle Giffords in Arizona, Paul Krugman wrote for the *New York Times*, "We don't have proof yet that this was political, but the odds are that it was."[47] Krugman defamed the Tea Party movement, Sarah Palin, and opponents of the 2010 Democratic health bill, falsely linking them to the murders. Krugman never did reveal his "proof," because the facts demonstrate his thesis was utterly groundless.

Sturgill might reply that these publications generally are good, and the problems I discuss mostly were corrected within the realm of journalism. We will return to the false claim of Sturgill's paper that "there is no recourse for bad journalism in the [Potter] series." Here the point is that, in real life, journalists often make mistakes (and sometimes they act unethically), and as children mature they should learn to interact with media critically rather than blindly assume it reflects some Platonic ideal.

Moreover, the fact that inaccuracies and errors within journalism are so often corrected demonstrates the importance of a critical readership. It is exactly the sort of critical, independent thinking exemplified by Harry Potter and his allies that serves to correct journalistic mistakes. Consumers of journalism will do well to adopt the thoughtful skepticism promoted by the Potter series.

Flawed Methodology Pulls Quotes Out of Context

The express methodology of Sturgill's paper is to take quotes from the Potter series out of the context of the story. However, it is only within the context of the story that the relevant quotes may be properly understood.

Sturgill's paper explains: "Two coders completed a framing analysis of the media references in the *Harry Potter* series of children's books. ...The coders were provided with an exhaustive compendium of direct quotes from the first six books of the series that made any mention of media." In other words, the "coders" utterly ignored the context of the quotes.

Moreover, all countervailing evidence to the paper's thesis was simply discarded from the "frames." The paper claims that "it was discovered that there were not enough references to Muggles' journalism for it to be used as a frame." However, even minor references to Muggle (non-magical) journalism are important, as they help establish the context for normal, non-magical life (i.e., our real world).

The paper continues:

> The only examples of news given are ones that portray it as manipulated, inaccurate and unethical. References to the Wizarding world's only other newspaper, the tabloid *The Quibbler*, and references to other forms of media such as radio were minor and not of any particular significance when weighed against the references made to corrupt, underhanded journalism.

The paper's claim about the *Quibbler* is simply false: the *Quibbler* publishes a key interview that dramatically impacts the progression of the story. (We will return to this important omission later.) Likewise, radio plays a pivotal role in the series in the final book, though Sturgill's paper addresses only the first six books. (The final Potter book was published in 2007, shortly before the release of Sturgill's article.)

Interestingly, Sturgill's paper notes three examples of honest journalism before dismissing those examples as irrelevant. For example, "In the first book, Harry, while at school, learns about a break-in at an important bank vault in the wizarding world."

Sturgill's paper, then, wrongly downplays the significance of brief instances of good journalism, which help set the context for a normal world; it omits very important instances of critical journalism (as we shall see later in more detail); and it misrepresents the significance of quotes that it does cover. I'll continue with that last point in discussing the character of Rita Skeeter.

Rita Skeeter's Role in the Novels

Critical to understanding the quotes about journalism are the plots of the novels. In *Goblet of Fire*, the character of Rita Skeeter serves several literary functions. First, she recognizes Harry as a celebrity and turns his story (or some fictionalized version of it) into gossip news.

Notice that, far from offering a distorted vision of how journalism actually operates, the Potter series describes how many journalists in fact tend to treat celebrities. Just look at how popular media treat the romantic relationships of famous movie stars. Look at the media's (and the public's) obsession with celebrities like Lindsay Lohan, Britney Spears, and so on. Look at the legions of paparazzi photographers who surround virtually every major celebrity. Thus, insofar as Skeeter represents a gossip columnist pandering to the prurient tastes of her audience, she simply mirrors how real-life journalism often functions.

Skeeter serves another function in the novel's story: she reveals how well-known people can be subject to fickle public sentiment. Recall that, as Harry enters the magical world, complete strangers approach him and praise him for defeating Voldemort (which Harry barely remembers, as it happened in his infancy). In the second novel, Harry is treated to the unfounded suspicions of his classmates, who fear his alleged connection to the monster roaming the school. In *Goblet of Fire*, Harry again experiences the ups and downs of public fame, and his experiences reflect those of many real-life public figures.

Skeeter also helps to set up Harry's crisis of confidence in Professor Dumbledore, which plays out over the final book.

It is Skeeter who writes the biased biography of Dumbledore that causes Harry to doubt his former mentor. Notably, in this biography Skeeter gets her facts basically right, only she fails to grasp the full context of Dumbledore's life that makes forgiveness of his worst actions (from his youth) possible.

Obviously Rowling does not intend Skeeter to represent the typical journalist of our world. Instead, Rowling uses Skeeter to advance several of the novels' story lines.

Context Matters: Voldemort's Rise to Power

Another of Skeeter's roles in the novels is to anticipate the growing problems with media in the wizard world, a significant concern of *Order of the Phoenix*. As Sturgill's paper intimates, a major theme of the novels, so far as media is concerned, is "government control of journalism."

It is on this point of government censorship that Sturgill and her coauthors completely fail to account for the purpose of the novels. The Potter novels are not merely fun stories of magic in which characters happen to populate successive books. Instead, the plot arc of the novels spans the entire series. Over the first three books, Voldemort plots his return to power. In the fourth book, he succeeds in regaining his powers. In the fifth book, the Ministry of Magic refuses to acknowledge his return to power and seeks to vilify Harry and his allies. It is in this context that the Ministry actively censors the press.

Over the span of the final two books, Voldemort seizes control of the Ministry. Voldemort, a brutal and murderous tyrant, in important ways mirrors the rise of Adolf Hitler. Under Voldemort's reign, the major media indeed become the government's propaganda machine. That Sturgill's paper simply ignores this plot arc is shocking.

In the final three books of the series, Rowling is not writing to represent the normal state of journalism; she is writing to show what happens to a society when its government becomes corrupt and then falls to the rule of a dictator. One implication of such a state of affairs is that journalism becomes subject to government manipulation and censorship.

Notice that journalism is not the only field subject to oppressive government controls: in *Order of the Phoenix*, the Hogwarts school falls under the corruptive influence of Ministry lackey Dolores Umbridge. The Minister of Magic subverts the criminal law itself by persecuting Harry over a bogus charge. (See Chapter Two and "Wizard Law and Segregation" in this book for further discussion of Ministry corruption.)

Does Sturgill wish to deny that corrupt governments often turn to censorship? Does she wish maturing children to ignore this crucial fact of history? Does she wish citizens to turn a blind eye to such problems because they do not fit neatly into coding frames?

Books about Nazi propaganda do not represent, and do not claim to represent, typical journalism in a healthy society. Neither do novels about the rise of a Hitler-like dictator, which is precisely what the Potter books are.

Context matters. Yes, particularly in the final books of the series, government agents defile the field of journalism. They do so in an era of government corruption and, eventually, dictatorship. Again the Potter books do not distort reality; they address real-life problems.

The *Quibbler*'s Pivotal Interview

As noted, Sturgill's paper refers to journalism in the *Quibbler* as "minor and not of any particular significance." The claim is ridiculous, given that the *Quibbler* publishes an interview with Harry of pivotal significance.

In *Order of the Phoenix*, Harry's ally Hermione Granger calls the *Quibbler* "rubbish," a well-deserved appraisal given its penchant for publishing sensationalistic, groundless stories. However, in the novel's frightening era of corrupt government and the accompanying censorship of the media, the *Quibbler* plays a crucial role in getting the truth out to the public.

Hermione conscripts Skeeter to write the "true story. All the facts. Exactly as Harry [a first-hand witness to the relevant events] reports them. ...I want to give him [Harry] the opportunity to tell the truth!" Rita replies, "There's no market for a story like that." Hermione retorts, "You mean the *Prophet* won't print it because Fudge [the Minister of Magic] won't let them."

Skeeter claims, "People just don't want to believe [Voldemort is] back." Hermione retorts, "So the *Daily Prophet* exists to tell people what they want to hear, does it?" Skeeter answers, "The *Prophet* exists to sell itself, you silly girl."

Sturgill's paper recounts the story to that point, but the paper declines to tell the rest of the story.

Luna Lovegood, daughter of the *Quibbler*'s editor, says of her father, "He publishes important stories that he thinks the public needs to know." Skeeter retorts, "I could manure my garden with the contents of that rag."

Hermione persists in her view that journalism can and properly does serve to tell the truth to the public. She tells Skeeter, "Well, this is your chance to raise the tone of it a bit, isn't it?"

Skeeter replies that nobody will take an article in the *Quibbler* seriously.

Hermione's reply is noteworthy:

> Some people won't. But the *Daily Prophet*'s version of the Azkaban breakout [in which Voldemort's followers escaped from prison] had some gaping holes in it. I think a lot of people will be wondering whether there isn't a better explanation of what happened, and if there's an alternative story available, even if it is published in...an *unusual* magazine—I think they might be rather keen to read it.

Once Skeeter agrees, Hermione says, "Okay, Harry? Ready to tell the public the truth?"

Hermione's views of journalism are precisely the opposite of what Sturgill's paper claims the series promotes. While Hermione rightly recognizes the dangers and shortcomings of government-controlled media, she also recognizes the crucial role journalism can play in relating the truth to the public.

While Skeeter suggests that newspapers focus on sensationalistic stories in order to sell copies to gullible readers, Hermione respects readers enough to realize that they are dissatisfied with obviously shoddy journalism, and generally they are intelligent enough to tell when a story rings true and when it does not.

For Sturgill's paper to fail to report Hermione's views of journalism, in a paper purportedly about the portrayal of journalism in the Potter series, is fantastically unprofessional and unjust toward Rowling's work.

While it is true that, within the unusual context of the series, Hermione conscripts Skeeter by threatening to expose her illegal means of gathering information, Hermione's lessons easily carry over to real life. Without Skeeter's assistance, Hermione could have found another writer to cover the story, or she could have written it herself. In our world, citizen journalists often write letters, op-eds, and blog posts to advance a story. While Sturgill's paper claims that Skeeter is the only "journalist of any consequence" named in the series, the claim is wrong: Hermione also functions as an important journalist—a citizen journalist—in this case.

Recourse to Bad Journalism

We have seen that Sturgill's paper is wrong to claim that, in the Potter series, "references to any form of accurate, non-obstructive journalism were virtually non-existent." Sturgill's paper also wrongly asserts that "there is no recourse for bad journalism in the series" and that bad "journalism always goes unpunished."

In addition to showing Hermione's role in publishing the interview with Harry, the novels portray a variety of other ways in which characters respond to and correct faulty journalism. Harry follows a variety of competing media outlets, including the *Daily Prophet* and the Muggle news, for hints about what's going on in the magical world. While *Deathly Hallows* lies outside the scope of Sturgill's paper, in that novel the *Quibbler*'s editor continues to report the truth (though he finally relents under Voldemort's threats), and Harry's allies use the radio to report the news of the resistance.

Personal contacts also serve an important role in spreading the truth and countering bad journalism. For example, after the *Quibbler*'s interview with Harry is published, Harry receives a stack of letters from readers. Some are unsupportive, but some recognize the truth of his account. One of Harry's classmates apologizes for not believing Harry and sends a copy of the *Quibbler* interview to his mother.

The students of Hogwarts flagrantly defy the Ministry's attempt to silence the truth. Dolores Umbridge, who has taken over the school, declares, "Any student found in possession of the magazine *The Quibbler* will be expelled." Hermione is thrilled by Umbridge's response, saying to Harry, "If she could have done one thing to make absolutely sure that every single person in this school will read your interview, it was banning it!" Obviously Hermione does not support Umbridge's authoritarian control of the school, but she rightly predicts her fellow students' response. Similarly, in our world, Banned Books Week promotes works that have been banned.[48]

Ultimately, the message of the Harry Potter series, in terms of journalism, is that the best way to fight bad journalism is to keep telling the truth. For example, finally in *Order of the Phoenix*, after the facts are too overwhelming even for the Ministry and the *Prophet* to ignore, the paper relents, reporting, "In a brief statement Friday night, Minister of Magic Cornelius Fudge confirmed that [Voldemort] has returned to this country and is active once more."

The Potter novels teach that, even in the face of shoddy reporting or outright censorship, the truth can prevail if its advocates keep fighting for it.

Truth in Journalism

Sturgill and her coauthors rightly urge educators and parents to "expose children to a wide variety of literature that demonstrates the essential role of journalism in a free society."

However, Sturgill's paper wrongly criticizes the Potter series for showing an "extremely negative depiction of journalism [that] could have an adverse effect on child readers." Ironically, Sturgill's paper employs Rita Skeeter's technique of dropping context and ignoring critical facts even as it wrongly accuses the Potter series of doing the same.

Rowling's works encourage children to think for themselves. (See also Chapter Two of this book.) The novels encourage readers neither to accept whatever they read or watch at face value, nor to uncritically reject it. Rather, the novels encourage readers to critically examine claims, regardless of their source, for internal consistency and adherence to the facts. Most importantly, the series urges readers to fight for the truth.

Essay Four

Beedle the Bard Expands Rowling's Moral Themes

J. K. Rowling's The Tales of Beedle the Bard *was published in 2008 by Children's High Level Group in association with Arthur A. Levine Books. Page numbers in this essay refer to that book. To evaluate the moral significance of the tales, important details about them must be revealed, so readers may wish to peruse the stories before returning to this essay.*

J. K. ROWLING'S *THE TALES OF BEEDLE THE BARD* postdates her seven-volume Harry Potter series and expands that universe. It is not a novel. Instead, it presents five short fairy tales beloved (in the Potter universe) by young witches and wizards. In her introduction, Rowling explains that the tales "have been popular bedtime reading for centuries, with the result that the Hopping Pot and the Fountain of Fair Fortune are as familiar to many of the students at Hogwarts as Cinderella and Sleeping Beauty are to Muggle (non-magical) children" (p. vii).

Why should children and adults read the new stories, whether readers hail from the magical world or the real one? In *Tales*, Rowling consciously offers morality stories for children; she intends the stories to offer guidance for the reader's behavior. Thus, the stories shed light on the moral messages of the Harry Potter series, and they offer children and their parents an opportunity to contemplate and discuss the themes of a new set of fairy tales.

The mythical background of the book appeals to fans of the novels. Beedle the Bard lived in the fifteenth century, and his stories are newly translated by Harry's good friend Hermione Granger. Moreover, Albus Dumbledore, headmaster of Hogwarts during most of Harry's stay there, offers extensive commentary on the stories. Thus, not only does Rowling present a new set of morality tales, but (through Dumbledore) she explains their intended meaning in depth.

The real background of the book offers its own insights into Rowling's moral commitments. Rowling originally hand-wrote six copies as thank-yous to friends associated with the Harry Potter novels. She sold a seventh copy at Sotheby's auction in London, where Amazon purchased it for nearly two million British pounds.[49] Rowling donated the proceeds to the Children's Voice Campaign, a project of the Children's High Level Group, a charity that she co-founded. Proceeds from the mass-produced hardback, as well as the limited run Collector's Edition (offered by Amazon), also fund the charity.

Baroness Nicholson of Winterbourne, who co-founded the charity with Rowling, explains in an afterword to *Tales*, "More than one million children live in large residential institutions across Europe," often without adequate nutrition, health care, education, or "emotional contact and stimulation" (p. 109). The charity aims to improve the conditions of these children and enable them to "live with families…or in small group homes" (p. 110).

Anyone who has read the Harry Potter series realizes that Rowling is very concerned with the well-being of children. Before he enters the magical world at the age of eleven, Harry himself suffers neglect and abuse. The charity, then, is a natural extension of Rowling's interests. It is also in line with the values of the major heroes of the novels. In her introduction, Rowling writes, "It is the belief of all who knew him personally that Professor Dumbledore would have been delighted to lend his support to this project, given that all royalties are to be donated to the Children's High Level Group, which works to benefit children in desperate need of a voice" (p. xii).

"The Wizard and the Hopping Pot"

Rowling's charitable cause relates to the theme of the first tale, "The Wizard and the Hopping Pot," though it is a shame that the story is not nearly as interesting as the book's real background.

The "Hopping Pot" involves the son of "a kindly old wizard who used his magic generously and wisely for the benefit of his [non-magical] neighbors" (p. 1). Not wanting to reveal his magical identity, the older wizard pretends his powers come from his "lucky cooking pot" or cauldron. His son, however, nurses his bigotry toward his Muggle neighbors. To counter this bigotry, before he dies the father places a spell on the cauldron, causing it to pester the son if he neglects to similarly care for his neighbors. Finally, with the pot driving him crazy, the son relents and starts helping his neighbors as his father did before him.

The problem with this tale—and I consider it the weakest of the lot—is that it mixes two distinct themes and fails to strongly develop either. Dumbledore tells us that only a "nincompoop" would take the significance of the story to be merely that a "young wizard's conscience awakes, and he agrees to use his magic for the benefit of his non-magical neighbors." (The young wizard helps his neighbors in order to avoid the pestering pot, not because of any awakened conscience.) Instead, Dumbledore argues, the real significance of the story is its opposition to bigotry against Muggles. Instead of showing Muggle sympathizers to be weak and stupid, the story shows "a Muggle-loving father as superior in magic to a Muggle-hating son" (p. 11). Anyone familiar with the novels knows that bigotry against Muggles is a major trait of the evil Lord Voldemort and his malicious followers.

What are we to make of the competing theme of charity? Unlike Rowling, who, after achieving great personal success, co-founded a charity close to her heart to help innocent children, the wizard's son chooses to help his neighbors just to keep the cauldron from bothering him. He hardly manifests a charitable spirit or pursues charitable work for good reasons.

A wizard might have various legitimate reasons to help his neighbors through magic (though Dumbledore reminds us that, in 1689, largely in response to Muggle persecution, the wizarding world imposed the International Statute of Wizarding Secrecy [p. 13]). The wizard might enjoy spending his extra time honing and perfecting his powers. The wizard might appreciate the friendship of his neighbors and desire to keep them safe from harm. Or the wizard might want to help maintain a peaceful and productive community to live in.

However, a wizard might also legitimately refrain from helping his neighbors. He might find more personally rewarding ways to spend his time and energy. He might fear turning his neighbors into thoughtless and unmotivated dependents. (Potential neighborly spite and persecution play no role in the story, though they might become serious problems in a closer-to-life scenario.)

Regardless, the son is not left free to make his own decisions, whether from good or base motives. Instead, the father essentially compels his son to help his neighbors. Thus, while in the context of Dumbledore's comments the story offers a (poorly developed) lesson against bigotry, it fails to say anything interesting about charity.

"The Fountain of Fair Fortune"

The second tale, "The Fountain of Fair Fortune" (my personal favorite) concerns three witches and a luckless knight who undertake the difficult journey to the lucky fountain. They find that the journey itself, not some magical fountain, creates their fortunes. The effect of the fountain will surprise no one familiar with the "lucky" potion that Ron Weasley drinks before winning a Quidditch match in *Half-Blood Prince*; neither the fountain nor Ron's drink performs its miracles through magic.

Beedle's story is so pleasant, and so unambiguously positive in its message, that little remains for a reviewer to say. Apparently

Dumbledore faces this problem in his own review, as he spends most of his commentary recounting a failed theatrical adaptation of the story at Hogwarts.

"The Warlock's Hairy Heart"

"The Warlock's Hairy Heart," the third story, offers the richest psychological complexity. The story begins: "There was once a handsome, rich, and talented young warlock, who observed that his friends grew foolish when they fell in love, gamboling and preening, losing their appetites and their dignity. The young warlock resolved never to fall prey to such weakness, and employed Dark Arts to ensure his immunity" (p. 43).

The warlock's solution is to physically remove his heart and lock it away, where it "slowly shrivels and grows hair, symbolizing his own descent to beasthood," Dumbledore tells us (p. 59).

Finally, the warlock decides to marry, not for love, but for social status and wealth (pp. 46–47). His intended talks him into putting his heart back into his chest. "But it had grown strange during its long exile, blind and savage in the darkness to which it had been condemned, and its appetites had grown powerful and perverse" (p. 51). Overcome with blind passion, the warlock attempts to win the heart of the maiden—by slicing it out of her chest, killing her. "Vowing never to be mastered by his own heart, he hacked it from his chest," joining the woman in death (p. 53).

At one level the story deals with the value of love and the foolishness of trying to protect one's self by forgoing love. The primary significance of the story, however, is its psychology, particularly its warning against repression. One cannot "master one's heart" by trying to sever one's emotional attachment to values. Instead, to the extent that one suppresses values, one tends to become overwhelmed by uncontrolled emotional outbursts and to substitute superficial exploits for genuine values. That is a sophisticated theme for children.

Unfortunately, the story offers few insights into how to distinguish between staying in control of one's emotions (a good thing) and repressing one's emotional commitment to legitimate values (a bad thing).

Nor does the story offer guidance for overcoming repression by adopting positive values. Only the most extreme cases of repression tend to result in a conclusion as tragic and horrific as the one of the story. In most cases, people can overcome repression and return to psychological health and a value-centered life.

Thankfully, because romantic love is so obviously a positive value that should not be repressed, and because the wizard takes repression to an extreme, Rowling's story illustrates the dangers of repression in a relatively clear-cut way.

"Babbitty Rabbitty and Her Cackling Stump"

Even though Rowling's novels are filled with political themes, "Babbitty Rabbitty and Her Cackling Stump" is the only tale from Beedle with an obvious political angle. A king wants to learn magic himself but stamp out magic elsewhere in the kingdom. A charlatan offers to teach the king magic—for a hefty fee, of course. The charlatan tells the king that his (fake) wand will work only "when you are worthy of it." The king behaves similarly to the emperor with no clothes: "Every morning the charlatan and the foolish King walked out into the palace grounds, where they waved their wands and shouted nonsense at the sky" (p. 64).

Eventually the king tires of the games and demands success—or else he will take the charlatan's life. The charlatan, though, has happened upon a true witch, Babbitty. He threatens to turn her over to the king's witch hunters unless she secretly helps the king perform magic.

At first the king appears to succeed, until he tries a spell that the witch cannot perform, raising a dead dog back to life. Fearing for his life, the charlatan exposes the witch, hoping to deflect any anger onto her. Finally Babbitty outsmarts both the king and the charlatan, protecting the magical community in the process.

"The Tale of the Three Brothers"

The detail about the dead dog provides a transition to the final story. Dumbledore writes, "It was through this story [about Babbitty] that many of us first discovered that magic could not bring back the dead...wizards still have not found a way of reuniting body and soul once death has occurred" (pp. 78–79). As I review in Chapter Five of this book, Rowling believes in an immortal soul, and the quest for earthly immortality (as opposed to an eternal afterlife) constitutes one of the key motivations of the villains in the Harry Potter series, known as the Death Eaters.

In *The Tales of Beedle the Bard*, however, Rowling concerns herself with the problem of dealing with death, not the question of how to prepare for some afterlife. This is especially obvious in the final story, "The Tale of the Three Brothers" (which plays a prominent role in the final novel, *Deathly Hallows*). The problem of dealing with death is separable from a belief in an immortal soul.

Three magical brothers use their powers to cross a dangerous river. Death, "angry that he had been cheated out of three new victims," tries to trick the brothers into risking their lives by accepting dangerous gifts (p. 88). The combative eldest brother asks for an all-powerful wand. After the wizard kills somebody in a duel and brags about his wand, another wizard slits his throat as he sleeps, stealing the wand.

The second brother asks for the "power to recall others from Death" (p. 89). Yet he can summon only a shadowy likeness of his beloved. Distraught, he takes his own life. Harry learns about such dangers from the Mirror of Erised in *Philosopher's Stone*, when he nearly becomes obsessed with viewing images of his deceased parents in the mirror.

The third brother "asked for something that would enable him to go forth from that place without being followed by Death"; Death offers "his own Cloak of Invisibility" (p. 89). The third brother lives a long, peaceful, and apparently contented life, as opposed to a life of violence or one of endless sorrow. (In the novels Rowling offers a much richer conception of the good life; see Chapter One of this book.)

These, then, are the lessons from Beedle the Bard. Do not succumb to bigotry. Make your own fortune rather than relying on blind luck. Pursue legitimate values rather than repressing them. Do not try to rule over others or trick them. Deal with death by making the best out of life, not through violence or passive sorrow. Those are good messages for children and adults alike.

With her new tales, Rowling offers another trip, however brief, into the magical world of Harry Potter. She also provides a new body of fairy tales that children will enjoy for generations.

Essay Five

The Fading Magic of Tolkien and Alexander

THE READER TURNS THE FINAL PAGES of any great work of literature with a melancholy heart. Yet the taste of that melancholy differs between the text of J. K. Rowling and that of other great works of fantasy. In Rowling's work, Harry Potter leaves the normal world to enter the magical world, and that magic remains always present. In the works of J. R. R. Tolkien and Newbery Medal winner Lloyd Alexander, the heroes enter life in a world of magic, but by the end of the novels the magic fades. Magic for Rowling means something different than it does in those other works.

In what way does the magic fade in the works of Tolkien and Alexander? Consider first the words of the great wizard Gandalf to Aragorn, the human king, in the final pages of *The Lord of the Rings*:

> This is your realm, and the heart of the greater realm that shall be. The Third Age of the world is ended, and the new age is begun; and it is your task to order its beginning and to preserve what may be preserved. For though much has been saved, much must now pass away; and the power of the Three Rings also is ended. And all the lands that

you see, and those that lie round about them, shall be dwellings of Men. For the time comes of the Dominion of Men, and the Elder Kindred shall fade or depart. ...I shall go soon. The burden must lie now upon you and your kindred.⁵⁰

In Alexander's *The High King*, after the heroes prevail over the forces of evil, those tied to magic must depart. Prince Gwydion tells the young hero Taran, who is destined for a similar role as Aragorn: "One task remains. The Sons of Don, their kinsmen and kinswomen, must board the golden ships and set sail for the Summer Country, the land from which we came." The bard Taliesin explains that "the Summer Country is a fair land, fairer even than Prydain, and one where all heart's desires are granted."⁵¹

As Arwen abandons her magical heritage to marry Aragorn in *The Lord of the Rings*, so Eilonwy must abandon hers to marry Taran. As Eilonwy contemplates the journey to the Summer Country, she complains about the bitter parting. Dallben asks her, "Do you truly wish to give up your heritage of enchantment?" She answers, "If enchantments are what separates us, then I should be well rid of them!" Dallben says she can use her magic ring to accomplish it; he encourages her, "Wish with all your heart for your enchanted powers to vanish." Only then can she marry Taran.⁵²

In these earlier works of fantasy, in the end the magical community leaves non-magical mortal men and lets them run things. While the natural world and the magical world commingle for an extended age, finally the magic leaves this world to reside only in some magical otherworld. The world of magic and the world of nature irrevocably part ways.

What does the fading magic in Tolkien and Alexander signify? In Tolkien's work, the disappearance of magic marks the elevation of the (non-magical) race of men. Gone is the magic of the elves and the wizards. Men must fend for themselves by their own means. For Alexander, the disappearance of magic also marks the advance of men, and more specifically it marks the adulthood of a single figure, Taran. The allegorical significance of this is straightforward: as people mature, as a culture and as individuals, they stop thinking about the world in terms of magical forces and start to understand it through reason and science. Magic exists only for an immature human culture or a child.

Rowling's magical world serves quite a different purpose, indicated by the fact that Harry leaves the normal world to enter the magical world, where he remains. Within the first dozen pages of *Harry Potter and the Sorcerer's Stone*, we discover that a magical world has long stood beside our own, in secret. Harry learns he is a wizard when Hagrid announces this fact and presents his invitation to the Hogwarts School of Witchcraft and Wizardry. At the end of the series, after Harry's allies defeat Voldemort, Harry and his friends continue to live in the magical world; the magic remains as strong as ever.

For Rowling, dabbling in magic is not a mark of immaturity. It is not the case that, as one matures, one "grows out of" magic. Instead, Harry is born with magic in him, and at Hogwarts he embraces that magic and celebrates his magical achievements. While Rowling creates a fictional divide between the magical world and the Muggle world, what is significant about her novels is that the heroes live in the magical world, embrace it, fight for it, and remain in it always.

In the works of Tolkien and Alexander, the story arc involves humans moving away from magic. In the books of Rowling, Harry moves into magic. In the earlier works, abandoning magic is a sign of maturity. In Rowling's works, embracing magic is the beginning of maturity.

What, then, does Rowling's magic mean? Obviously Rowling does not wish us to believe that wizards really exist or that we can learn to cast spells. But she does wish us to hold close the deeper magic of the novels. We are not supposed to grow up and cast off magic, but rather learn how to fill our lives with the real magic of the stories.

What is that deeper magic? As I write in Chapter One of this book, Harry leaves "a deprived life with his awful uncle and aunt" and discovers "a new world…in which he is able to discover and actively pursue opulent values" (see page 16 of this book). Harry develops deep friendships with Hagrid, the Weasley family, and Hermione. He loves Sirius Black as his godfather and finds a mentor in Dumbledore. He discovers a loyal and heroic friend in Dobby. As he matures, his relationship with Ginny Weasley develops into romantic love. Harry also enjoys developing his magical abilities by playing Quidditch and learning defensive magic. He finds a new home in Hogwarts. He is passionate about his friends, his studies, his hobbies, and his life in the magical world.

Rowling's deeper magic is available to us all. All of Harry's values have analogs in our world: friendship and love, studies and schools, families, careers, liberty, sports, and laughter. I write in an earlier section, "As Muggles, we are not destined to fly by broom, duel with wands, or ride dragons. Yet the deeper magic of Harry Potter flows through our world, too" (see pages 97–98 of this book).

The melancholy of Tolkien's finale involves a sense of loss of the youthful period of our race. Once we walked with elves and wizards, once we witnessed the world of magic, but no more. Alexander likewise leaves behind the magic of youth; one must forsake magic to enter adulthood.

The final pages of Rowling's series, like those of the earlier fantasies, evoke the sorrow of leaving behind familiar friends. Now the stories of Harry Potter and his allies have reached their final page, where the reader is forced to acknowledge that after all Harry is ink and paper, not flesh and blood. Yet, because Rowling's magical world lives on within the fiction, it inspires the reader to keep actively in mind the deeper magic that Harry discovers.

While magic wands remain beyond our grasp, we can share the true magic of Harry Potter if only we will reach out to it with a welcoming hand.

Essay Six

Harry Potter's Lessons for Muggle Politicians

A version of this essay originally appeared in the Rocky Mountain News *just prior to the 2008 elections.*[53]

HARRY POTTER INSPIRES READERS OF ALL KINDS. As we approach an important election, what lessons do these British books hold for American politicians?

Do the right thing even if it's difficult. Harry's mentor, Professor Dumbledore, tells his students that they must sometimes "make a choice between what is right and what is easy."

Entitlements offer a prime example. Social Security's trustees report that "the cost of Social Security will generally increase faster than the program's income" for decades to come as more people retire and live longer and fewer people have children.[54] It's easy to ignore the problems, pitch trivial fixes, or weakly promise to soak the rich. That course is irresponsible.

Be honest even when it's inconvenient. When the Minister of Magic asks Harry to "stand alongside the Ministry" to "give the right impression," Harry responds angrily. Not only did the Ministry long deny the truth about Voldemort's threat, but it locked up an innocent person to look tough.

In the Muggle world, both supporters and opponents of the Iraq war could agree the Bush administration overemphasized weapons of mass destruction and neglected to communicate other reasons for going to war.

Don't cling to power. Dumbledore urges the minister to "send envoys to the giants," long abused by the magical community, before Voldemort recruits them. The minister whines that "people hate them . . . end of my career." Dumbledore fires back, "You are blinded by the love of the office you hold!"

While candidates sincerely disagree on many issues, too often they are tempted to put power first. For example, politicians routinely load up spending bills with pork for local supporters.

Government is not always the answer. Dumbledore's Order of the Phoenix battles Voldemort while the Ministry officially denies the threats and smears Dumbledore. The Weasley family needs no government program to invite Harry into their home, and, later, Harry in turn offers a helping hand to the son of a fallen ally.

Independent businesses, not politicians, drive production of the goods and services we need to thrive. Politicians will disagree about welfare policy, and the Potter books offer no advice on the matter. They do show, however, that family and friends provide crucial support systems. (Elsewhere Rowling has endorsed government programs addressing poverty and even lionized socialist Jessica Mitford, but these political views play no obvious role in the novels.[55])

Sometimes government gets it wrong. The Ministry resorts to censorship, politically motivated prosecutions, imprisonment on pretense, and political manipulation of Harry's school. It sanctions elf slavery and finally falls under Voldemort's influence. Harry and his allies defy the Ministry and practice civil disobedience to protect the innocent.

While our government is usually better, it once protected slavery and racist laws, censored the press, and took political prisoners (see the Alien and Sedition Acts). Today the government sometimes limits free speech, and it prohibits many voluntary exchanges.[56]

While the Potter books take a direct stand only on select political matters, they do clearly warn us to be careful with government power.

Government should protect people's rights. The Aurors compose the respected police force that helps fight Voldemort's forces. The wizards' government protects against the Unforgivable Curses that control, harm, or kill others.

Our laws protect people from similar uses of force. As any newspaper reports on any day, Muggles don't need wands to hurt others. Governments properly act to protect people from criminal harm. Whatever other debates capture the attention of politicians, they ought not lose sight of that central function.

Give us substance, not empty rhetoric. The Harry Potter books reveal deep political themes, yet they resist politicization.

Just as writers should take care not to claim Harry Potter's sympathy with views on which the books are silent, so politicians should be careful to claim they are working in the mold of JFK, Reagan, FDR, or Thomas Jefferson.

Dumbledore offers outstanding closing advice for everyone interested in politics: "It takes a great deal of bravery to stand up to our enemies, but just as much to stand up to our friends."

Essay Seven
Why Potter Fans Should Read Ayn Rand

A version of this article originally appeared in Grand Junction Free Press.⁵⁷

I HAVE LONG BEEN A FAN OF AYN RAND'S WORKS. When I was young, my father read aloud *Anthem* as a bedtime story. *Anthem* is Rand's novelette about a dystopian future in which people are known by numbers, not names, and the word "I" has been outlawed. The hero of the story rediscovers electricity in secret and eventually escapes with his beloved to freedom. The book helped inspire my preoccupation with liberty.

More recently, I grew passionate about another novelist: J. K. Rowling, author of the Harry Potter series, and that passion led to this book about Rowling's themes of the heroic valuer, courage, independence, and free will.

This shared passion for Rand and Rowling is no coincidence. The two authors explore many of the same themes and offer their readers gripping, tightly plotted stories filled with great heroes, dastardly villains, and intriguing ideas. Fans of Rowling easily could fall in love with Rand's works, and vice versa.

Both novelists have written great Romantic works. In her introduction to *The Fountainhead*, Rand writes that Romanticism "deals, not with the random trivia of the day, but with the timeless, fundamental, universal problems and *values* of human existence" (see page 97 of this book). That helps explain why Rand's books remain strong sellers decades after their initial release and why Rowling's books appeal to readers across continents speaking many languages. These are not stories of the neighbor next door and his neuroses. These are grand epics of monumental clashes between good and evil.

As heroic valuers, Harry and his allies fight courageously to protect their lives, loved ones, futures, and liberties from the vicious tyrant Lord Voldemort. For example, in *Sorcerer's Stone*, Harry gives a fiery speech to his friends Ron and Hermione, persuading them to take action against Voldemort to save their lives and world.

Rand's characters, too, fight passionately for their values. In *The Fountainhead*, Howard Roark refuses to compromise his integrity as an architect, even if that means he must work in a granite quarry or blow up a building that has ripped off and debased his design. In *Atlas Shrugged*, John Galt and Francisco d'Anconia walk away from their normal lives in order to finally subvert the evil men and ideas taking over the world.

After learning he's a wizard, Harry takes the Hogwarts Express to a magical world filled with wonder, possibility, and great champions like Professor Dumbledore. Hogwarts is Harry's escape from the oppressive Dursleys. In *Atlas Shrugged*, Dagny Taggart's Transcontinental Railroad also symbolizes movement into a world of near-mythical champions such as the steel-producer Hank Rearden.

While Harry has Hogwarts, Dagny discovers Galt's Gulch, the place where her heroes live. After Dagny crash-lands her plane in the Gulch, she experiences, "This was the world as she had expected to see it at sixteen…This was her world, she thought, this was the way men were meant to be and to face their existence."[58] It is to this spirit of youthful passion and confidence that both novelists remain true.

As Rand explains, free will is the foundation of Romantic literature, because free will is what enables a person's "formation of his own character and the course of action he pursues in the physical world."⁵⁹ Because of the fact of free will, people can form or reform their characters and act for their values. This is the premise behind any compelling plot, which depends on the characters making and then enacting choices toward some goal. It is no surprise, then, that Dumbledore endorses free will, saying "it matters not what someone is born, but what they grow to be."

Rowling and Rand share an interest in other themes as well. Both authors love liberty and hate tyrants; both John Galt and Harry Potter work outside the established government to fight those wielding power corruptly. Both authors present fiercely independent heroes who refuse to unquestioningly follow self-proclaimed authorities.

Of course the writers also have their differences. For example, while Rand solidly rejects religion, Rowling includes the Christian elements of self-sacrifice and life after death in her novels. Yet the writers' similarities are more intriguing.

These novels open the door to enthralling and potentially life-altering adventures. You have the power to discover your own Hogwarts or Galt's Gulch, not merely in the realm of imagination, but in your daily life.

Essay Eight

Reflections on Films Six and Seven

My wife and I saw the film *Harry Potter and the Half-Blood Prince*, the sixth film of the series from Warner Brothers, opening night. The theater lobby was filled with plenty of capes and other magical paraphernalia. A couple of young blokes loudly held mock magical duels. I feared the audience would be too raucous and unruly for me to hear all the dialog, but that wasn't a problem. People were there to enjoy the movie, and they respected other people's viewing. There was a bit of audible crying during—well, you know. Overall it is a fine movie that does well by the book.

I remain disappointed by some of the film's omissions. True, adapting a lengthy and complex novel for cinema requires cutting down the amount of material. However, the movie substantially weakens some of the book's themes by dropping important scenes.

The love theme is much stronger in the book than it is in the movie. Love is a crucial theme of the book: Narcissa Malfoy shows her love for her son, various heroes become romantically involved, and Dumbledore explains the troubled love that Voldemort's mother Merope develops for his Muggle father.

Unfortunately, what the movie omits leaves that theme underdeveloped. We get the main romantic developments between Harry and Ginny as well as between Ron and Hermione. But the film does not include the romances between Lupin and Tonks (who make brief appearances) or Bill Weasley and Fleur. Nor does the movie reveal the tragic history of Voldemort's parents.

Most disappointing to me personally is the film's omission of the Minister of Magic's visit with Harry, a scene that sharply illustrates Harry's devotion to Dumbledore. In the novel, the minister asks Harry to "stand alongside the Ministry" to "give the right impression," and the minister mocks Harry's loyalty to Dumbledore. Harry responds angrily, proudly proclaiming to be "Dumbledore's man through and through." This is my favorite scene of the book, particularly as it does so much to establish the relationship between Harry and Dumbledore, and I regard its omission in the movie as a tragedy.

The movie includes the scene of Dumbledore's death but changes it from the book. The major and most troubling change of that scene is that, in the film, Dumbledore does not freeze Harry to keep him safe, as he does in the novel. Instead, Harry waits below, watching dumbly. That was a mistake because it makes Harry look weak, and it removes one of the important acts that Dumbledore takes to protect his beloved student.

The final major omission is the fight scene at Hogwarts near the end of the story. In the book, this is where Bill becomes disfigured by Greyback, leading to Fleur lovingly standing by him. In the movie, the villains basically waltz away, though at least Harry puts up some resistance.

On the whole, though, the movie is true to its medium; it interprets the story for film. The actors, including the three leads, perform well; as always, Alan Rickman mesmerizes as Snape. The reaction of the students and faculty to Dumbledore's death is visually stunning and emotionally powerful.

The film does not and cannot recreate the book exactly as written for the screen. For the most part the film skillfully adapts the story for a very different medium; only in a few cases do the changes and omissions damage the story. True, the film feels largely like a bridge work between the fifth and seventh installments, but that is the nature of this part of the story. (The film might have been aptly titled "Voldemort Strikes Back.") On the whole the film does justice to the novel.

Deathly Hallows: Part I

Harry Potter and the Deathly Hallows: Part I is a good movie but not a great one. My favorite remains the highly stylized *Prisoner of Azkaban*, the only Potter film directed by Alfonso Cuarón. While I enjoyed *Hallows I*, it seemed to me both disjointed and emotionally muted.

Part of the difficulty is that *Hallows I* loses several of the series' finest actors. Alan Rickman remains spectacular as Snape, but he has a small role in the movie. Michael Gambon, who had finally won me over in his role as Dumbledore after the unfortunate demise of Richard Harris, is gone (except for brief images) due to his character's death in the previous film. (If Gambon at times plays Dumbledore too aggressively, Harris perhaps gave the role too soft a touch.) Gone are the delightfully funny Emma Thompson as the batty Trelawney and the appropriately stern Maggie Smith as Professor McGonagall. Also assigned to bit parts are David Thewlis (Remus Lupin), Brendan Gleeson (Mad-Eye Moody), and Jason Isaacs, who does a spectacular job as an off-the-rails Lucius Malfoy.

To me, though, the best actor of the series has been Gary Oldman as Sirius Black, who portrays the warm, charming, protective, and reckless godfather to Harry. He is a major reason (besides the outstanding direction) that I love the third film so much, and he adds both sparkle and tragedy to *Order of the Phoenix* (my second-favorite film of the series). There is simply no mature actor in the latest film with enough screen time to provide such a cornerstone.

Bill Nighy held promise as Minister of Magic Rufus Scrimgeour, but unfortunately the filmmakers undercut that role by minimizing the tensions between Scrimgeour and Potter. They might as well have left out the role completely, as much as I like Nighy, and saved the time for more important scenes.

Much more of the weight of this latest film, then, rests on the shoulders of Daniel Radcliffe, Rupert Grint, and Emma Watson as Harry, Ron, and Hermione. And generally they do a fine job. Grint impresses with his meanness and Watson with her forlorn longing. The two together create a compelling romantic couple. Unfortunately, Watson just doesn't persuade me that she is viciously tortured by Bellatrix Lestrange. Nor does Radcliffe quite convey the deep sense of loss and fury over losing his friend in what should have been the movie's finale.

And what happened to the terrifying Helena Bonham Carter as Lestrange? In this film she seems more pathetic than scary, perhaps because she overplays her sycophantic overtures to Voldemort, and again, most of the torture scene seems scary but less than horrifying. Voldemort (Ralph Fiennes) too falls short of his terrifying potential.

The filmmakers seem reluctant to let go of the children's series and fully embrace the adult themes of the final Potter novel. As another example, they minimize the physical trauma of the Weasley brothers Bill and George. Bill, who was supposed to have played a role in *Half-Blood Prince* but was unfortunately omitted from the film, shows up here with minor scarring on his face, otherwise looking gorgeous. That's wrong. Bill becomes grotesquely deformed in the sixth novel, and turning that into a couple of scars both minimizes the danger of Voldemort's forces and undercuts Fleur's loving devotion for him. Nor does George's head wound seem as traumatic as it does in the novel.

Or consider Umbridge's inquisition of the "mudblood" in the Ministry's lower chambers. In the book this scene imposes psychological terror. In the film the situation seems merely unpleasant. Nor does this sequence show the others brutally treated by the Ministry or their heroic rescue by the three leads.

There is a counterexample, however. When Ron ends up "splinched"—partly torn apart due to a bad magical transport—his pain seems both believable and terrifying. The success of the scene depends largely on the skill of Grint, who finally gets the chance to prove he can do more than look befuddled or frightened.

I regard it as close to a cinematic sin that Lupin does not visit Harry at the Black residence. Not only would that scene have given one of the series' mature actors a larger presence in the film, it would have established Harry's growing maturity and his deep commitment to parental bonds (for, as readers of the novel will recall, Harry demands that Lupin return to his pregnant wife). Moreover, the scene would have added another dimension to the problem of bigotry that Harry confronts, for Lupin, as a werewolf, suffers severe bigotry from others.

The filmmakers botch the ending by leaving off with Voldemort capturing the Elder Wand from Dumbledore's grave. This dampens the significance of the funeral of Dobby, the courageous elf.

The filmmakers could have instead planted the seeds for Voldemort's quest for the wand (one of the three Hallows), then drawn more from the novel to spin out the tension between Harry and Hermione over whether to go after Horcruxes or Hallows. In the novel, Dobby's death has a way of clarifying the issues for Harry, which resolves Harry's tensions with his friends, and that is entirely absent from the film. Dobby remains a great character in the movie, but his death is not the epic finale, the catharsis, the turning point, and the moment of clarification that it could have been and should have been.

Even though I dislike some of the filmmakers' choices, some of them are inspired. The way the film introduces Dobby works well, even though it varies from the novel. The animated retelling of "The Tale of the Three Brothers," the story about the Deathly Hallows, is both mesmerizing and important to the film. And the film does a fine job dealing with the bigotry of Voldemort's forces. Another very nice touch is the dance between Harry and Hermione, which effectively offsets (and therefore emphasizes) their general state of misery. Finally, the cinematography is stunning, particularly involving the landscapes.

While the film gets quite a lot right, it misses a number of opportunities to achieve the dark tone and emotional devastation of the novel. Thus, the film does not provide the contrast needed to fully bring out the story's struggling hopes. Overall, though, the film remains a fine addition to a charming series that fans of Rowling's work will continue to watch far into the future.

Notes

References to J. K. Rowling's books follow the numbered notes and appear in the order used in this book, denoted by an abbreviated quote or description. Page numbers for this book appear in bold. In a few instances capitalization varies from the books. The citations use abbreviated book titles as indicated below. Arthur A. Levine Books is an imprint of Scholastic Press.

Stone: J. K. Rowling, *Harry Potter and the Sorcerer's Stone* (New York: Arthur A. Levine Books, 1998).

Chamber: J. K. Rowling, *Harry Potter and the Chamber of Secrets* (New York: Arthur A. Levine Books, 1999).

Prisoner: J. K. Rowling, *Harry Potter and the Prisoner of Azkaban* (New York: Arthur A. Levine Books, 1999).

Goblet: J. K. Rowling, *Harry Potter and the Goblet of Fire* (New York: Arthur A. Levine Books, 2000).

Phoenix: J. K. Rowling, *Harry Potter and the Order of the Phoenix* (New York: Arthur A. Levine Books, 2003).

Prince: J. K. Rowling, *Harry Potter and the Half-Blood Prince* (New York: Arthur A. Levine Books, 2005).

Hallows: J. K. Rowling, *Harry Potter and the Deathly Hallows* (New York: Arthur A. Levine Books, 2007).

Numbered Notes

1. Scholastic, "Scholastic Announces Record Breaking Sales of 11.5 Million Copies of Harry Potter and the Deathly Hallows in First Ten Days," August 2, 2007, http://www.scholastic.com/aboutscholastic/news/press_08022007_CP.htm.

2. Julie Mollins, "Bible Is America's Favorite Book: Poll," *Reuters Life*, April 8, 2008, http://www.reuters.com/article/lifestyleMolt/idUSN0835916320080408.

3. Scholastic, "New Study Finds That the Harry Potter Series Has a Positive Impact on Kids' Reading and Their School Work," July 25, 2006, http://www.scholastic.com/aboutscholastic/news/press_07252006_CP.htm.

4. BBC News, "Chancellor Praises Potter Books," July 14, 2005, http://news.bbc.co.uk/2/hi/entertainment/4683219.stm. This source and the last one were provided by Wikipedia at http://en.wikipedia.org/wiki/Harry_Potter.

5. WorldNetDaily.com, "Witchcraft in America: Behind the Growing Fascination with All Things Pagan, Occult and Magic," January 2, 2008, http://wnd.com/news/article.asp?ARTICLE_ID=59488. The attribution claimed by the cited article has not been verified.

6. The quote about *Jesus Camp* is included on my blog post, "Religious Insanity," January 10, 2008, http://www.ariarmstrong.com/2008/01/religious-insanity.html. The documentary's web page is http://www.jesuscampthemovie.com/.

7. Cindy Wooden, "Writers in Vatican Newspaper Debate Lessons of Harry Potter Novels," Catholic News Service, January 15, 2008, http://www.catholicnews.com/data/stories/cns/0800250.htm. This source was provided by Wikipedia at http://en.wikipedia.org/wiki/Religious_debates_over_Harry_Potter.

8. Ayn Rand, *The Fountainhead* (New York: Bobbs-Merrill Company, 1971). In the novel, Howard Roark epitomizes independence in thought and action, while Peter Keating acts as an extreme version of a second-hander.

9. For more on the Dursleys' self-deception, see Diana Mertz Hsieh, "Dursley Duplicity: The Morality and Psychology of Self-Deception," *Harry Potter and Philosophy: If Aristotle Ran Hogwarts*, ed. David Baggett and Shawn E. Klein (Chicago: Open Court, 2004), pp. 22–37.

10. Clarence Darrow, "Closing Argument: The State of Illinois v. Nathan Leopold & Richard Loeb," August 22, 1924, http://www.law.umkc.edu/faculty/projects/ftrials/leoploeb/darrowclosing.html.

11. Leonard Peikoff, *Objectivism: The Philosophy of Ayn Rand* (New York: Dutton / Penguin Group, 1991), pp. 56–57.

12. Joel Achenbach and Dale Russakoff, "Teen Shooter's Life Paints Antisocial Portrait," *Washington Post*, April 29, 1999, http://www.washingtonpost.com/wp-srv/national/daily/april99/antisocial04299.htm.

13. *The New Oxford Annotated Bible: Revised Standard Version* (New York: Oxford University Press, 1973), p. 1310 (John 15:12–13).

14. Dave Kopel, "Deconstructing Rowling," *National Review Online*, June 9, 2003, http://www.nationalreview.com/kopel/kopel062003.asp.

15. John Granger, *Looking for God in Harry Potter* (Carol Stream, IL: SaltRiver Books / Tyndale House Publishers, 2004), pp. 19, 61.

16. Aristotle, "Nicomachean Ethics," *The Complete Works of Aristotle: The Revised Oxford Translation*, vol. 2, ed. Jonathan Barnes, trans. W. D. Ross and revised by J. O. Urmson (Princeton, NJ: Princeton University Press, 1984), p. 1825 (Book VIII, Section 1).

17. Aristotle, pp. 1827–28 (Book VIII, Section 3).

18. Aristotle, p. 1852 (Book IX, Section 12).

19. Aristotle, pp. 1849–50 (Book IX, Section 9).

20. *The New Oxford Annotated Bible*, p. 1289 (John 3:16).

21. Ayn Rand, "The Ethics of Emergencies," *The Virtue of Selfishness* (New York: Signet, 1964), p. 44. Rand also uses the example of the penny and dollar in John Galt's speech in *Atlas Shrugged* (New York: Signet, 1992), p. 953. Both passages are also included in *The Ayn Rand Lexicon* at http://www.aynrandlexicon.com/lexicon/sacrifice.html.

22. Aristotle, p. 1829 (Book VIII, Section 5).

23. Aristotle, pp. 1846–48 (Book IX, Section 8).

24. Aristotle, p. 1788 (Book V, Section 5).

25. *The New Oxford Annotated Bible*, p. 1177 (Matthew 5:39, 5:44).

26. I do not mean to imply here that Christians necessarily are pacifists. As Dave Kopel writes in his working paper, "Evolving Christian Attitudes Towards Personal and National Self-Defense," November 27, 2007, http://davekopel.com/Religion/Evolving-Christian-Attitudes.pdf, "In the nineteenth and early in the twentieth centuries, the traditional Christian concepts of Just War and of the individual's duty to use force to defend himself and his family remained uncontroversial, as they had been for centuries." Nevertheless, Christianity clearly promotes self-sacrifice in general and opens the door to sacrificing one's self for one's enemies. This remains in sharp contrast with the views of Aristotle and Rand.

27. The Wikipedia entry on Draco Malfoy proved a useful reminder of this citation as well as the one about "Malfoy's gaunt, petrified face"; see http://en.wikipedia.org/wiki/Draco_Malfoy.

28. Darla Graff, who reviewed parts of this book, made this point in personal correspondence.

29. *Telegraph*, "J. K. Rowling: 'Christianity Inspired Harry Potter,'" October 20, 2007, http://www.telegraph.co.uk/arts/main.jhtml?xml=/arts/2007/10/20/bopotter120.xml.

30. Ayn Rand, *The Fountainhead*, p. v.

31. For the essays in the Expanded Edition, Melissa Holt assisted with editing, Ed Peters helped edit and check citations, and Jennifer Armstrong reviewed the text and formatted it.

32. J. K. Rowling quoted in Adeel Amini, "Minister of Magic," *Student*, March 4, 2008.

33. Stuart MacDonald, "I Contemplated Suicide, Says Harry Potter Creator, JK Rowling," *Times*, March 23, 2008, http://entertainment.timesonline.co.uk/tol/arts_and_entertainment/books/article3602774.ece; Stephen McGinty, "The JK Rowling Story," *Scotsman*, June 16, 2003, http://news.scotsman.com/jkrowlingharrypotter/The-JK-Rowling-story.2436228.jp. Ed Peters encouraged more detailed research on the timeline of Rowling's depression, and Wikipedia helped with tracking down the second citation of this note.

34. Stephen McGinty, "The JK Rowling Story."

35. Martyn McLaughlin, "JK Rowling: Depression, the 'Terrible Place that Allowed Me to Come Back Stronger,'" *Scotsman*, October 2, 2010, http://news.scotsman.com/jkrowlingharrypotter/JK-Rowling-Depression-the-39terrible.6561855.jp.

36. Stuart MacDonald, "I Contemplated Suicide, Says Harry Potter Creator, JK Rowling."

37. "J. K. Rowling: A Year In the Life, Part 2," *ABC News*, July 16, 2009, http://abcnews.go.com/video/playerIndex?id=8105333.

38. Adeel Amini, "Minister of Magic," *Student*, March 4, 2008.

39. J. K. Rowling, *The Tales of Beedle the Bard* (New York: Children's High Level Group and Scholastic Inc., 2008), p. 13.

40. J. K. Rowling, *The Tales of Beedle the Bard*, p. 12. See also Chamber 150.

41. J. K. Rowling, *The Tales of Beedle the Bard*, p. 13.

42. Amanda Sturgill, Jessica Winney, and Tina Libhart, "Harry Potter and Children's Perceptions of the News Media," *American Communication Journal*, vol. 10, issue 1, Spring 2008. The article is no longer available through the online link created by the journal. The essay in this book draws on an archive of the online article that lacks page references. For more information about the journal article, see the release from Baylor University (where Sturgill lectured), "Newspapers Already Struggling—and 'Harry Potter' Doesn't Help," July 29, 2009, http://www.baylor.edu/pr/news.php?action=story&story=59849.

43. "'Potter' Bad for Newspapers?", *UPI*, July 30, 2009, http://www.upi.com/Entertainment_News/2009/07/30/Potter-bad-for-newspapers/UPI-74141249012677/.

44. Ari Armstrong, "ADL, *Denver Post* Defame Bob Glass," *Colorado Freedom Report*, May 29, 2001, http://www.freecolorado.com/2001/05/seibert.html.

45. Dan Barry, *et al.*, "Correcting the Record: Times Reporter Who Resigned Leaves Long Trail of Deception," *New York Times*, May 11, 2003, http://www.nytimes.com/2003/05/11/us/correcting-the-record-times-reporter-who-resigned-leaves-long-trail-of-deception.html.

46. Dave Kopel, "Too Often a Crutch," *Rocky Mountain News*, March 8, 2008, http://www.rockymountainnews.com/news/2008/mar/08/kopel-too-often-a-crutch/.

47. Paul Krugman, "Assassination Attempt in Arizona," *New York Times*, January 8, 2011, http://krugman.blogs.nytimes.com/2011/01/08/assassination-attempt-in-arizona/.

48. "Banned Books Week: Celebrating Freedom to Read," American Library Association, http://www.ala.org/ala/issuesadvocacy/banned/bannedbooksweek/index.cfm.

49. "Amazon to J. K. Rowling: Thank You," Amazon.com, http://www.amazon.com/gp/feature.html?ie=UTF8&docId=1000179911.

50. J. R. R. Tolkien, *The Lord of the Rings* (New York: Houghton Mifflin, 1994), pp. 949–50 ("The Steward and the King" in *The Return of the King*).

51. Lloyd Alexander, *The Prydain Chronicles* (New York: Guild America Books, 1973), pp. 688–89 (the final pages of *The High King*).

52. Lloyd Alexander, *The Prydain Chronicles*, pp. 700–701.

53. Ari Armstrong, "Lessons for U.S. Politicians from the Hogwarts School of Witchcraft and Wizardry," *Rocky Mountain News*, September 14, 2008, http://www.rockymountainnews.com/news/2008/sep/14/armstrong-lessons-for-us-politicians-from-the-of/.

54. "The 2010 Annual Report of the Board of Trustees of the Federal Old-Age and Survivors Insurance and Federal Disability Insurance Trust Funds," August 9, 2010, p. 20, http://www.ssa.gov/oact/tr/2010/tr2010.pdf.

55. Regarding Rowling's support for the Labour Party's policies on poverty, see Ben Leach, "Harry Potter Author JK Rowling Gives £1 Million to Labour," *Telegraph*, September 20, 2008, http://www.telegraph.co.uk/news/newstopics/politics/labour/3021309/Harry-Potter-author-JK-Rowling-gives-1-million-to-Labour.html. Regarding Rowling's interest in Mitford, see Lindsey Fraser, "Harry and Me," *Scotsman*, November 9, 2002, http://www.scotsman.com/jkrowlingharrypotter/Harry-and-me.2376441.jp. Ed Peters pointed out Rowling's interest in Mitford, and Wikipedia helped with tracking down both the citations used in this note.

56. For examples, see Timothy Sandefur, *The Right to Earn a Living* (Washington, D.C.: Cato Institute, 2010).

57. Linn and Ari Armstrong, "Why Harry Potter Fans Should Read Ayn Rand," *Grand Junction Free Press*, September 1, 2008, http://www.gjfreepress.com/article/20080901/COLUMNISTS/808319989/1021.

58. Ayn Rand, *Atlas Shrugged* (New York: Dutton, 1992), pp. 701–2.

59. Ayn Rand, "Free Will," *Ayn Rand Lexicon*, http://aynrandlexicon.com/lexicon/free_will.html.

Harry Potter Citations

Introduction
11. "Fear of a name"…Stone 298
"great deal of bravery"…Stone 306
"well-organized mind," "knack of choosing"…Stone 297
"Your mother died"…Stone 299

Chapter One
14. Hagrid rides…Stone 14
16. "like a slug"…Stone 22
"Harry Hunting"…Stone 31
"Dudley's gang hated"…Stone 30
Hagrid, the gamekeeper of Hogwarts, tells Harry…Stone 47–60
Harry meets the Weasley family…Stone 93–94, 98
17. "Voldemort's coming back"…Stone 270

18. Sirius was best friends…Prisoner 379, 432
"Sirius is trapped"…Phoenix 734
19. Luna has lovingly painted…Hallows 417
Like Harry, Neville suffered…Goblet 595
their first flying lesson…Stone 148–49
"You've got to stand up," "You're worth twelve"…Stone 218
"got no brains"…Stone 222–24
an escaped troll…Stone 175–76
20. "if Harry Potter only knew"…Chamber 177–78
magical bonds of slavery…Chamber 14
"burst into tears"…Chamber 13
Harry tricks Lucius…Chamber 338
21. "cunning folk"…Stone 118 (italics removed)
"Slytherin will help you"…Stone 121
"no good and evil," "He does not forgive"…Stone 291
bodily host…Stone 293
22. "left Quirrell to die"…Stone 298
"you never did anything"…Prisoner 370
"what was there to be gained"…Prisoner 374
"Only innocent lives," "should have died"…Prisoner 375 (emphasis removed)
state of perpetual terror…Goblet 9–11
chop off his own hand…Goblet 641–42
"uncontrollable weeping"…Goblet 645
new hand…Goblet 649
strangles him…Hallows 470
23. "things worth dying for"…Phoenix 477
"my only son"…Prince 33–34
"those who were left were slain"…Hallows 549
"obvious instincts for cruelty"…Prince 276–77
"a half life"…Stone 258
24. "an act of violation"…Prince 497–98
"mutilated beyond the realms"…Prince 502
25. "protected by an ancient magic"…Phoenix 835–36
"could have forced her"…Hallows 344 (italics removed)
26. Draco confronts Dumbledore…Prince 591, 595–96
"ripped apart"…Hallows 683
Dumbledore is severely injured…Prince 580
a previous injury…Hallows 681
27. "fragment of soul"…Hallows 686
"not supposed to survive"…Hallows 691
he remembers a kiss…Hallows 704
Dumbledore suspected…Hallows 708–10

Chapter Two
29. "funny clothes"…Stone 3
Vernon tries to pretend…Stone 4

Notes

"imagining things"…Stone 5
30. "Mrs. Next Door's problems"…Stone 6
"Uncle Vernon's new company car"…Prisoner 3
"pretended she didn't have a sister"…Stone 2
"perfectly normal"…Stone 1
"The Dursleys shuddered"…Stone 2
"we'd stamp it out"…Stone 53
"abnormality"…Chamber 2 (emphasis removed)
"squash the magic"…Prisoner 2–3
shower their son…Stone 21
he proceeds to destroy them…Stone 37
strange and abnormal…Stone 53
"Lily this and Lily that"…Stone 53
31. "sort of servant," "the other sort"…Stone 77–78
surrounds himself with pictures…Chamber 119
book-signing event, "front page"…Chamber 59–60
gives his students a test…Chamber 99–100
detention…Chamber 120
32. "Celebrity is"…Chamber 120
brags about his skills…Chamber 141
removes all the bones…Chamber 173
make a snake disappear…Chamber 194
"My dear boy," "you've just been taking credit"…Chamber 297
33. resigns from the school…Prisoner 423
poor spirits, in love with Lupin…Prince 623–24
marriage with Lupin…Hallows 46
"I'm pretty sure my father"…Hallows 212
"I made a grave mistake"…Hallows 213
"I'd never have believed this"…Hallows 214
34. announces the birth…Hallows 514
"deeply boring book," "got it all planned out"…Chamber 58
35. "Mr. Crouch is quite right"…Goblet 141
"Percy ought to have realized"…Phoenix 71
"Fudge only wants"…Phoenix 72
"determined to start a panic"…Goblet 707
"envoys to the giants"…Goblet 708
36. "Fudge thinks"…Phoenix 93
"Ministry's leaning heavily"…Phoenix 94
37. Fudge falsely calls…Phoenix 142
"The Ministry does not have"…Phoenix 149
"it's all perception"…Prince 344–45
"You see, I don't like"…Prince 346–47
38. physically abuses Harry…Phoenix 266–67
"forming his own"…Phoenix 303
"High Inquisitor"…Phoenix 306
breaking his followers out…Phoenix 544

guards under his control…Phoenix 558
Umbridge first appears…Phoenix 146–47
39. "never knew I ordered"…Phoenix 747
"Are you a Ministry-trained"…Phoenix 242
Umbridge calls Harry a liar, "I saw him"…Phoenix 245
40. "Senior Undersecretary"…Hallows 250
Umbridge falsely accuses…Hallows 257–61
41. "The Dark Lord's word"… Prince 32
"Harry, obedience is a virtue"…Goblet 662
"I can make bad things"…Prince 271
"was already using magic"…Prince 276
Riddle dislikes his first name…Prince 274–75
"There he showed his contempt"…Prince 277
42. "liked to collect"…Prince 277
"Voldemort had committed"…Prince 439
"another of Hogwarts's founders"…Prince 440
Unforgivable Curses…Goblet 212–15
"ornately carved thrones"…Hallows 241–42
43. "Imagine how he will reward me"…Goblet 678
Bellatrix becomes incensed…Phoenix 784
"most loyal servant"…Phoenix 811
"do not punish me"…Phoenix 812 (emphasis removed)
"He calls me his most loyal"…Prince 29
does not prevent Voldemort…Hallows 549
"My Lord"…Hallows 724
44. "You will hear many of his Death Eaters"…Prince 277
"No, master!"…Goblet 138
Later we find Dobby…Goblet 375–76
"Dobby hasn't found work"…Goblet 378
45. "Dobby likes being free"…Goblet 378
Dumbledore agrees to accept them, "Winky is properly ashamed"…Goblet 379
"barmy old codger"…Goblet 380
Hermione publicly upbraids…Goblet 138
"unswerving obedience," "His *slave*"…Goblet 154
hours in the library…Goblet 198
S.P.E.W., "They *like* being enslaved"…Goblet 224
"they're *happy*," "uneducated and brainwashed"…Goblet 239
46. "The fates have informed me"…Prisoner 296
"Not that ridiculous Grim," "I'm leaving!"…Prisoner 298
"It means the Ministry's interfering"…Phoenix 214
Umbridge commands the students…Phoenix 240
"Harry could not remember," "Did you want to ask," "Well I don't"…Phoenix 241
47. "I've already read," "what Slinkhard says"…Phoenix 316
"But I disagree," "Well, I'm afraid"…Phoenix 317
"learn Defense"…Phoenix 325
"I thought it would be good"…Phoenix 339

NOTES

"I'm feeling a bit"…Phoenix 634
"It's no wonder"…Stone 172
48. "she's got no friends"…Stone 172
"bossy sort of voice," "not very good"…Stone 105
"You're saying it wrong"…Stone 171
other people's business…Stone 110
teacher's pet…Stone 137
an escaped troll…Stone 175–78
"I think he's brilliant"…Stone 78
49. Harry meets Draco, "I think I can tell"…Stone 108–9
"simply to trust"…Hallows 563

Chapter Three
52. "*Not Slytherin*," "Well, if you're sure"…Stone 121
"There are strange likenesses"…Chamber 317
"You happen to have many qualities," "put me in Gryffindor"…Chamber 333
"purity of blood"…Goblet 708
"make a choice"…Goblet 724
53. nailed a snake…Prince 201
attacking the official…Prince 202
54. "Muggles and filth"…Prince 203
"defeated looking person," "sack of muck"…Prince 205
nearly strangles her…Prince 207
Morfin informs Gaunt, "dirty-veined Muggle"…Prince 210 (emphasis removed)
Gaunt again tries to strangle…Prince 210–11
sentenced to Azkaban…Prince 211–12
"alone and free," love potion…Prince 213
Dumbledore speculates…Prince 214
"came staggering up"…Prince 266
"a fresh leaf"…Prince 361
Voldemort murders his father…Prince 366–67
56. "yer a wizard"…Stone 50
"I'm a *what*?"…Stone 51
Harry's jaw drops…Stone 52
"horrible mistake"…Stone 57
Harry recalls…Stone 58
Riddle tries to magically control…Prince 269–70
57. "I can make things move"…Prince 271
"I knew I was different"…Prince 271
"Filth!"…Phoenix 78 (emphasis removed)
58. "because I hated"…Phoenix 111
"they thought Voldemort"…Phoenix 112
Sirius's relatives Bellatrix…Phoenix 113–14
shabbily dressed…Hallows 663
Snape befriends Lily…Hallows 664, 666
resists the prejudices…Hallows 666

fighting parents...Hallows 667
Snape causes a branch to fall...Hallows 668
look down on Petunia...Hallows 671
He feels jealous...Hallows 674
59. His friends...Hallows 673
finally join with Voldemort, "in his humiliation"...Hallows 675
Snape joins the Death Eaters, prophesy...Hallows 677
"He has her eyes," "If you loved Lily"...Hallows 678
"Look...at...me"...Hallows 658
Albus Severus...Hallows 758
60. "Muggles forced," "had a few scruples"...Hallows 716
"Dumbledore gave a little gasp"...Hallows 717
"arrogance and stupidity"...Hallows 718
the aged prisoner, "They say he showed remorse"...Hallows 719
"think about what you've done"...Hallows 741
61. "it was possible that he felt sorry"...Prince 361
62. "noted for a vein"...Prince 212
64. "books written about Harry Potter"...Stone 13
He throws tantrums...Stone 21, 23
poke people with a stick...Stone 33
no correction or guidance...Stone 31
"the appalling damage"...Prince 55
Dudley takes Harry's advice...Hallows 35
Dudley shows genuine concern...Hallows 38–40
65. "arrogant little berks," "best friend"...Phoenix 670–71
heads of his dead ancestors...Phoenix 62
"alone too long"...Phoenix 110
66. "Kreacher is what he has been made"...Phoenix 832
past vicious treatment of Kreacher...Hallows 196–200
Kreacher finally begins to help...Hallows 219–21, 225
Kreacher leads the elves...Hallows 734
67. "High above them"...Goblet 119
Ron is subjected...Prince 390–92
"They took my Luna"...Hallows 419
69. "closer than a son"...Goblet 678
"had never loved"...Goblet 684
"There is no good and evil"...Stone 291

Chapter Four
72. "Your mother died"...Stone 299
77. "Not my daughter"...Hallows 735–36 (emphasis removed)
78. "You've got to make some sacrifices!"...Stone 283
Nicolas Flamel...Stone 220
"he and his wife will die"...Stone 297
"I am sorry"...Hallows 700
79. tiara or diadem, "If we die for them"...Hallows 627–34 (emphasis removed)

NOTES

80. "I'm about to kill you," "My dear boy"...Prince 591
"feel my wrath"...Hallows 174
"Draco's expression"...Hallows 458–59
Draco grows up...Hallows 756
81. the diadem disintegrates...Hallows 635
"Is Draco alive?"...Hallows 725–26 (italics removed)
82. "It destroyed her," "because if the Ministry"...Hallows 564–65
"I resented it"...Hallows 715–16
83. St. Mungo's as a caring facility...Phoenix 505–6, 512–15
84. "I wanted glory"...Hallows 716
Grindelwald, "Wizard dominance"...Hallows 357 (italics and emphasis removed)
"weapon that would lead us to power"...Hallows 716
teaching at Hogwarts...Hallows 718
Dumbledore defends his brother...Hallows 566–67

Chapter Five
86. thirty-seven presents...Stone 21
proceeds to destroy...Stone 37
87. Hagrid as a servant...Stone 78
Draco's first major confrontation...Stone 148
"chocolate cake"...Stone 47–48
"mounds of gold coins"...Stone 75
considers buying...Stone 80–81
88. wand...Stone 81–85
"He knew he was being stupid"...Prisoner 183
When Ron complains...Stone 100
89. "magpie-like tendency"...Prince 276–77
90. Voldemort kills...Prince 439
"A Horcrux is the word"...Prince 497–99
91. "preferred objects with a magical history"...Prince 503–4
92. "to the well-organized mind"...Stone 297
The ghost tells Harry...Phoenix 861
"if I picked up a sword"...Hallows 104
"The last enemy"...Hallows 328
94. the evil of killing a unicorn...Stone 258
"nothing worse than death"...Phoenix 814

Conclusion
96. "To Miss Hermione Jean Granger"...Hallows 125–26 (emphasis removed)
Minister Scrimgeour assumes...Hallows 126
"curled up"...Hallows 316
"humans are frightened of death"...Hallows 426

The Psychology of Harry Potter
101. "Its face"...Prisoner 83
102. "I felt weird"...Prisoner 85
"freezing water"...Prisoner 178–79

"dementors affect you," "darkest, filthiest places"...Prisoner 187
"Dementor's Kiss"...Prisoner 247
103. Harry seeks Lupin's help...Prisoner 239, 243
"slab of chocolate"...Prisoner 84
A Patronus...Prisoner 237
"very happy memory"...Prisoner 237–38
memories of his father...Prisoner 240
"silver shadow"...Prisoner 241–42
"not a shapeless cloud"...Prisoner 411–12
104. "the dead we loved"...Prisoner 427–28
"shape-shifter"...Prisoner 133
"best to have company"...Prisoner 134
105. "riddikulus"...Prisoner 134
his grandmother's clothes...Prisoner 135
mummy...Prisoner 137–38
werewolf...Prisoner 138
her own children...Phoenix 175–76
"I'm impressed"...Prisoner 155
106. "heart's desire"...Stone 207–9
"nothing to stop him"...Stone 212
"happiest man," "Men have wasted away"...Stone 213
107. "dwell on dreams"...Stone 214
wizard photographs...Stone 304
"the second brother"...Hallows 407, emphasis removed
"he lived alone"...Hallows 408–9, emphasis removed
108. "curiously shaped cut"...Stone 15
"sharp, hot pain"...Stone 126
"a pain like he'd never felt"...Stone 256
"it's a warning"...Stone 264
"about to split in two"...Stone 294
agonizing pain...Stone 294–95
"leaves its own mark"...Stone 299
109. hear a voice...Chamber 120
scene of a crime...Chamber 137–39
snake language...Chamber 195–96
"strange likenesses"...Chamber 317
"his own powers," "It is our choices"...Chamber 333
Harry grows so angry...Phoenix 8
110. "consumed with anger"...Phoenix 42
yells at them...Phoenix 65–66
"insides burn"...Phoenix 76
Harry lashes out...Phoenix 235, 244
"made his scar prickle"...Phoenix 118, 329
When Harry is awake...Phoenix 380–81
"*Why* did he know"...Phoenix 384
dreams he is a snake...Phoenix 462–63

Index

Alexander, Lloyd, 139–42
American Communication Journal, 120–30
ancient magic, 25, 75
Aristotle, 12, 72–74, 76, 77, 89, 97, 157
Aurors, 116, 145
authority, 29, 36, 39–43, 46, 47, 49
Avada Kedavra, 42, 67, 79
Azkaban prison, 38, 54, 82, 101
Bible, 9, 10, 71, 74, 77, 96
bigotry (*See* prejudice)
Black, Regulus, 66
Black, Sirius, 14, 18, 19, 22, 23, 33, 38, 53, 57–59, 61, 65, 66, 68, 72, 73, 92, 111, 142
Black, Walburga (mother of Sirius and Regulus), 57, 65
Blair, Jayson, 121
blood traitors, 42, 49, 57
boggarts, 104–6
broomstick, 17, 18, 72, 79, 87, 88, 97 (*See also* Quidditch)
Catholicism, 10, 71 (*See also* Christianity)
Catholic News Service, 10, 71
censorship, 36, 67, 125, 129, 144
centaur, 23, 93
charity, 132–34
chess, 78
children (*See* youth)
choice (*See* free will)

Christ (*See* Christianity; Jesus)
Christianity, 10, 12, 14, 17, 71, 72, 74–78, 85, 86, 95, 96, 148, 157
Columbine High School, 69
consciousness, 55, 56, 61, 63, 89–91, 94, 95
control (*See* power; Unforgivable Curses; Voldemort)
courage (*See* heroism)
cowardice, 22, 32, 33, 68, 93
Crabbe, Vincent, 79–81
cross, 74, 77, 95 (*See also* Horcrux)
Crouch, Barty, Jr., 43, 68, 69
Crouch, Barty, Sr., 34, 35, 44, 45, 69
Cruciatus Curse, 42, 43, 67, 79, 84
culpability, 26, 51, 60–69, 80
Daily Prophet, 36, 127, 129 (*See also* censorship)
Dark Arts, 17, 46, 47 (*See also* Horcrux; Unforgivable Curses)
Darrow, Clarence, 55
death, 107, 137
  cursed life worse than, 24, 90, 93, 94
  fear of, 12, 86, 89–91, 93, 95, 96
  values in the face of, 24, 26, 27, 71, 74, 91, 95
  villains cause own, 21–24, 77
  (*See also* immortality; murder)
Death Eaters, 43, 44, 58, 59, 67, 90, 92 (*See also* Crabbe, Vincent; Crouch, Barty, Jr.; Lestrange,

Bellatrix; Malfoy, Lucius; Malfoy, Narcissa)
deception (*See* dishonesty)
dementors, 33, 38, 39, 64, 101–4
Denver Post, 121–22
dependence, 29–44, 48–50, 66 (*See also* independence)
depression, 100–104, 114
dishonesty, 30, 32, 35–40, 49, 60, 66, 68, 69, 156 (*See also* honesty)
Divinations, 46
Dobby, 20, 21, 44, 45, 49, 53, 66, 67, 72, 111–12, 153
dragon, 11, 96, 117
Dumbledore, Aberforth, 82–85
Dumbledore, Albus, 45, 59, 63, 78, 96, 97, 132–37, 142–45
  beliefs of, 11, 53, 92
  death of, 23, 25, 26, 58, 71, 77, 80, 150
  Harry Potter and, 49, 64, 66, 72, 73, 83, 108–12, 150
  Ministry of Magic and, 35–39, 116
  Voldemort and, 23–25, 27, 41, 42, 44, 52–54, 56, 57, 61, 62, 72, 90, 91, 94
  youth of, 60, 80, 82–85, 124–25
Dumbledore, Ariana, 60, 63, 82–85
Dumbledore's Army, 47
Dursley, Dudley, 16, 30, 31, 38, 56, 64, 65, 86–89
Dursley, Petunia, 10, 16, 29–31, 56, 58, 64, 86–89, 156
Dursley, Vernon, 10, 16, 29, 30, 36, 56, 64, 86–89, 98, 156
elf (*See* Dobby; Kreacher; slavery; Society for the Promotion of Elfish Welfare; Winky)
enemies, 11, 27, 74, 77, 79, 95, 157
envy, 30
ethics (*See* morals)
facts, 28, 29, 35–40, 47, 49, 62, 95
fame, 31, 49, 50, 64
Firenze, 23, 93
first-handers (*See* independence)
Flamel, Nicolas, 78

force, 16, 20, 22, 25, 30, 34, 38, 40–42, 49, 60, 66–68, 80, 86, 157
  (*See also* power; Unforgivable Curses)
Franks, Bobby, 55
freedom (*See* free will; liberty)
free will, 11, 12, 50–70, 147
friendship
  independence and, 11, 28, 31, 35, 48–50, 58, 94
  sacrifice and, 71, 79
  value of, 11, 15–19, 24, 25, 27, 56, 65, 68, 72–74, 76–78, 83, 87–89, 91, 95, 97
  villains and, 21–23, 41, 44, 59
Fudge, Cornelius, 35–39, 52, 115, 127
Gaunt, Marvolo, 53, 54, 63
Gaunt, Merope, 54, 57, 62, 63, 65, 67
Gaunt, Morfin, 53, 54, 63
giants, 35, 62, 116, 144
Glass, Bob, 121
goblins, 116
Gospel of John, 71, 74 (*See also* Bible)
Gospel of Matthew, 77 (*See also* Bible)
Goyle, Gregory, 79–81
Granger, Hermione, 53, 62, 92, 96, 97, 116, 126–29, 132, 142
  Harry Potter and, 17–19, 49, 66, 72, 73, 78, 79, 81
  independence and, 39, 44–48, 94
Granger, John, 71
Grindelwald, Gellert, 60, 84, 85
Gryffindor, 21, 52
Hagrid, Rubeus, 14, 16, 31, 48, 56, 62, 72, 87, 88, 142
Hallows, 96–98, 107, 137–38, 153
Harris Poll, 9
Harry Potter and the Chamber of Secrets, 18, 20, 31, 52
Harry Potter and the Deathly Hallows, 9, 20, 66, 97, 107, 129, 151–54
  (*See also* Hallows)
Harry Potter and the Goblet of Fire, 11, 124
Harry Potter and the Half-Blood Prince, 23, 25, 26, 53, 58, 80, 134, 149–51

Harry Potter and the Order of the Phoenix, 18, 57, 92, 125–26, 129
Harry Potter and the Prisoner of Azkaban, 22, 68, 101
Harry Potter and the Sorcerer's Stone, 10, 21, 72, 77, 92, 97, 137, 141 (*See also* Philosopher's Stone)
Harry Potter books
  Christian criticism of, 10, 12, 71
  literacy and, 9, 10, 13
  popularity of, 9, 14, 15, 50, 72, 98
  (*See also individual titles*)
heroism
  free will and, 51, 53, 58
  loyalty and, 20, 82
  readers and, 13, 97, 98
  sacrifice and, 12, 74, 75, 77–79, 82, 83, 85, 86, 95
  values and, 11–17, 21, 24, 25, 27, 37, 72, 77, 85, 87, 91, 93, 94, 98
  (*See also* independence)
Hitler, Adolf, 11, 125–26 (*See also* Nazis; World War II)
Hogwarts, 44–46, 58, 66, 79, 92, 116
  Harry Potter and, 16, 17, 21, 30, 34, 37, 87, 89
  staff and, 26, 31, 32, 38, 84
  Voldemort and, 42, 52, 54, 56, 57, 61
honesty, 29, 36, 37, 39, 40, 44 (*See also* dishonesty)
Horcrux, 12, 23, 79, 90, 91, 94, 95, 112
Hsieh, Diana, 156
imagination, 14, 29, 44, 97
immortality, 11–13, 70, 71, 74, 85, 86, 90–95, 98 (*See also* death)
Imperius Curse (*See* Unforgivable Curses)
independence, 11, 12, 28, 29, 34, 39, 40, 43–50, 65, 66, 70, 94, 95, 98
International Statute of Wizarding Secrecy, 115, 117, 134
Jesus, 10, 71, 74, 77, 95, 96 (*See also* Christianity)
Jesus Camp, 10, 156

journalism, 11, 36, 67, 68, 120–30
King's Cross, 16, 60
Kopel, Dave, 71, 122, 157
Kreacher, 65–67
Krugman, Paul, 122
law, 11, 37, 38
Leopold, Nathan, 55
Lestrange, Bellatrix, 23, 43, 44, 58, 77
Lewis, C. S., 71
liberty, 11, 18, 24, 44, 45
Lockhart, Gilderoy, 31, 32
Loeb, Richard, 55
Longbottom, Frank and Alice, 19, 83
Longbottom, Neville, 18, 19, 83, 87
Looking for God in Harry Potter (Granger), 71
love
  families and, 53, 83–85, 88
  friends and, 15, 18, 19, 27, 56, 72, 73, 75, 76, 89
  immortality and, 91, 93
  objects and careers, 26, 49, 50, 72
  parents and, 25, 27, 74, 77
  romantic, 27, 33, 54, 59, 62, 67, 72, 97, 135–36, 149
  sacrifice and, 10, 70, 72, 74, 77, 95
  villains and, 21, 23, 24, 36, 43, 44, 69, 72, 91
  (*See also* friendship; parenthood)
Lovegood, Luna, 18, 19, 67, 68, 127
Lovegood, Xenophilius, 67, 68, 129
love potion, 54, 67
Lupin, Remus, 32–34, 36, 49, 58, 63, 72, 73, 78, 88, 102–5, 116, 153
Malfoy, Draco, 19, 20, 23, 26, 31, 48, 49, 52, 53, 57, 64, 65, 79–82, 87–89, 94
Malfoy, Lucius, 20, 23, 53
Malfoy, Narcissa, 23, 53, 58, 81, 82
materialism, 86–91, 94, 95 (*See also* possessions)
McGonagall, Minerva, 64
Ministry of Magic, 34–40, 42, 43, 45, 46, 53, 54, 72, 82, 125–27
Mirror of Erised, 106–7, 137
morals, 89, 93

free will and, 51–53, 63, 65, 67, 69, 80, 98
friends and, 19, 35, 48, 58, 73, 74, 88, 95
Harry Potter books and, 13, 96, 97
independence and, 11, 28, 29, 44
sacrifice and, 12, 75, 78, 81, 83
values and, 13, 15, 27, 91, 98
(*See also* heroism; independence; values)
Mudblood, 42, 49, 59
Muggles, 31, 40, 42, 43, 49, 50, 52–54, 58, 60, 62, 63, 65, 67, 84, 97, 117–19
murder
Draco attempts, 23, 26, 80
objects and, 42, 90, 91, 94
Potters suffer, 16, 18, 25, 30, 52, 59
real-life, 55, 69
rips the soul, 24, 26, 90
villains seek to, 18, 22, 23, 27, 37, 43, 54, 56, 58, 60, 67, 68, 79, 81, 84, 91, 92
(*See also* Unforgivable Curses)
narcissism, 31, 57
Nazis, 11, 40, 126
New York Times, 121–22
Nicholson, Baroness of Winterborne, 132
Nicomachean Ethics (*See* Aristotle)
Objectivism (*See* Peikoff, Leonard; Rand, Ayn)
objects (*See* possessions)
Order of the Phoenix, 22, 33, 35, 36, 57, 65 (See also *Harry Potter and the Order of the Phoenix*)
pain (*See* torture)
parenthood, 18, 23, 25, 26, 33, 34, 54, 61, 64, 72, 74, 75, 80, 86, 88
Parselmouth, 52
Passion (*See* cross)
Patronus charm, 103–4
Peikoff, Leonard, 61
persecution (*See* torture)
Pettigrew, Peter, 22, 23, 53, 68, 76
Philosopher's Stone, 17, 21, 78

Pope, 10
possessions, 12, 30, 31, 42, 86–91, 93, 94 (*See also* materialism)
Potter, Harry, 14, 22, 31, 43, 50, 66, 69, 128
childhood of, 10, 16, 17, 29, 30, 56, 64, 86
dementors and, 101–3
friends of, 19, 20, 45–48, 58, 67, 68, 72, 73, 92, 96
independence of, 32–34, 38, 40, 44, 47–49, 51–53
law and, 117, 126
Ministry of Magic and, 36, 37, 39
parents of, 25, 26, 59, 65, 72, 75, 92
sacrifice and, 79–83
scar and, 108–13
values of, 11, 15–18, 21, 24, 56, 77, 78, 87–89, 93, 94
Voldemort and, 23, 24, 27, 41, 54, 56, 57, 60, 71, 90
(*See also* Harry Potter books; Potter, James; Potter, Lily)
Potter, James, 16, 18, 25, 30, 33, 57–59, 65, 104, 116
Potter, Lily, 11, 16, 18, 25, 26, 30, 31, 57–59, 71, 72, 74, 75, 77, 102, 112
poverty, 58, 73, 88
power (over others), 10, 21, 32, 34, 35, 44, 49, 56, 67–69, 87
Dumbledore and, 84, 85
Ministry of Magic and, 36–40
Voldemort and, 19, 20, 24, 40–43, 57, 89
(*See also* force; Unforgivable Curses; Voldemort)
prejudice, 11, 16, 31, 33, 36, 45, 49, 52, 53, 57, 58, 62, 65, 80, 133–34
prophecy, 25, 59
publishing (*See* journalism)
pure blood, 42, 54, 58
Quibbler, 123, 126–29
Quidditch, 9, 17, 24, 49, 67, 73, 88, 89, 102, 134
Quirrell, 21, 22, 69, 108

www.ingramcontent.com/pod-product-compliance
Lightning Source LLC
LaVergne TN
LVHW051600070426
835507LV00021B/2680